# A VERY SHORT,
# FAIRLY INTERESTING AND
# ASONABLY CHEAP BOOK ABOUT
# MANAGEMENT

SECOND EDITION

# A VERY SHORT,
# FAIRLY INTERESTING AND
# REASONABLY CHEAP BOOK ABOUT
# MANAGEMENT

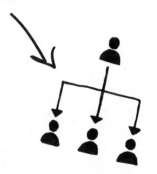

# ANN L. CUNLIFFE

Los Angeles | London | New Delhi
Singapore | Washington DC

Los Angeles | London | New Delhi
Singapore | Washington DC

SAGE Publications Ltd
1 Oliver's Yard
55 City Road
London EC1Y 1SP

SAGE Publications Inc.
2455 Teller Road
Thousand Oaks, California 91320

SAGE Publications India Pvt Ltd
B 1/I 1 Mohan Cooperative Industrial Area
Mathura Road
New Delhi 110 044

SAGE Publications Asia-Pacific Pte Ltd
3 Church Street
#10-04 Samsung Hub
Singapore 049483

Editor: Kirsty Smy
Editorial assistant: Nina Smith
Production editor: Sarah Cooke
Copyeditor: Gemma Marren
Proofreader: Fabienne Pedroletti-Gray
Marketing manager: Alison Borg
Cover design: Wendy Scott
Typeset by: C&M Digitals (P) Ltd, Chennai, India
Printed and bound by CPI Group (UK) Ltd,
Croydon, CR0 4YY

The title for the 'Very Short, Fairly Interesting and
Reasonably Cheap Book about...' series was devised
by Chris Grey. His book, *A Very Short, Fairly
Interesting and Reasonably Cheap Book about
Studying Organizations*, was the founding title of this
series.
Chris Grey asserts his rights to be recognised as
founding editor of the 'Very Short, Fairly Interesting
and Reasonably Cheap Book about...' series.

**Library of Congress Control Number: 2013947987**

**British Library Cataloguing in Publication data**

A catalogue record for this book is available from
the British Library

ISBN 9781446273500
ISBN 9781446273517 (pbk)

This book is dedicated to my daughter Lauren,
who also never takes the easy road and who I love dearly.

And to my grandson, Jamie, who I hope will follow the
road less travelled.

# Contents

# About the Author

Ann Cunliffe is Professor of Organization Studies at the University of Leeds. She previously held positions at the University of New Mexico, California State University, the University of New Hampshire, USA and the University of Hull, UK. She is also a Visiting Professor at Fundação Getulio Vargas, Brazil and the University of Strathclyde, Scotland.

Ann's current research interests lie at the intersection of organizational studies, philosophy and communications, to examine how organizational life, identities and action are shaped in living conversations. In particular, she is interested in exploring how we can engage in collaborative, responsive and ethical ways of managing organizations. Other interests include: leadership; self-work; sensemaking; collaboration; developing reflexive approaches to management research, practice and learning; and expanding the reach and 'rigour' of non-positivist qualitative research.

Her recent publications include the co-authored book *Key Concepts in Organization Theory* with John Luhman (2012), and articles in *Organizational Research Methods*, *Human Relations*, *Management Learning*, the *Journal of Management Studies*, and *Organization Studies*. In 2002 she was awarded the Breaking the Frame Award from the *Journal of Management Inquiry* for 'the article that best exemplifies a challenge to existing thought'.

Ann is currently joint Editor-in-Chief of the international journal *Management Learning* and Consulting Editor of *Qualitative Research in Organizations and Management*. She is a member of eight international editorial boards, was Division Chair of the Critical Management Studies Division of the Academy of Management (2010) and organizes the biennial Qualitative Research in Management and Organization Conference.

She received her PhD and MPhil from Lancaster University, UK.

# Acknowledgements

Chris Grey came up with the idea of a *Very Short* ... book, a readable yet challenging, easily carried book, discussing aspects of organizations not normally covered in textbooks or in the popular press. This different kind of book caught on, and I was fortunate to be given the opportunity to write the *Very Short* book on management in 2009. So my first acknowledgement goes to Chris for his brainwave. I was even more fortunate to be given the chance to write this second edition. Why? Because it's a great opportunity to include what I missed in the first edition, to rethink and update ideas and to try to make these challenging ideas even more accessible and relevant – I believe they are incredibly important if managers are to be effective and responsible citizens of a global society.

As with the first edition, the book seems to write itself, no matter how precise a plan I start with, because I encounter so many thought-provoking and engaging ideas. And once you start thinking about the possibilities those ideas offer ... well, they take you down some interesting paths! So I'm indebted to Kirsty Smy at Sage for her support and perseverance, and to the anonymous reviewers who provided constructive comments, many of which are embedded somewhere in the second edition. They were helpful beyond my expectations and I'll gladly buy you dinner if you identify yourself when we meet!

I'd especially like to thank colleagues and close friends including John Shotter, Karen Locke, Helen Muller and my WKA chums across the world whose inspiration and unfailing support and friendship over the years have kept me travelling along the paths I'm passionate about. And to my students and new colleagues at the University of Leeds.

As with the first edition, a special mention must go to all the students, who over the years have grappled with many of the ideas in this book, debated them, offered examples of their relevance and of how they've used them in their everyday management practice. Their insights have helped me articulate, refine and situate the notion of relational, reflexive and ethical managers – and will continue to do so.

Finally, to my parents for believing in me and for always being there.

Ann
New Mexico, 2013

# Why Should You Buy This Book?

Who is it for?

- Students of management, business studies, public and health care administration who want to understand management from different perspectives.
- Postgraduate students who have experience working in organizations and realize that managing is not as easy as most textbooks make out.
- Managers who want to read something that is both intellectually challenging and useful.
- Academics who are interested in less conventional ideas about management and who want ideas for challenging conversations with students.

Why buy it?

- You think there's something more to management than 5 Steps, SWOTs, Maslow, LMX, institutional theory and lists of principles.
- You want a different way of thinking about and doing management and being a manager.
- You are fed up with all those self-assessment questionnaires designed to make you a better manager.
- You work for someone who has an MBA and always does great on all those self-assessment questionnaires – yet still manages to irritate the heck out of everyone at work.
- You want to think more critically about management and managing.
- You like challenges.
- You are about to get on a seven hour flight to goodness knows where, you've forgotten your iPad and your only other options are romantic novels or autobiographies of people you've never heard of.

And if you do buy it and want to discuss anything, please email me at a.l.cunliffe@leeds.ac.uk.

# Introduction

Most management books cover topics such as finance, marketing, operations management, motivation, teamwork, project management, performance management, etc. To write yet another book addressing such topics seems to me to defeat the purpose of the *Very Short ...* series, because writing about 'business as usual' or 'management in five easy steps' tells us nothing new. Nor does it cause us to consider alternative views and perspectives that can lead to more ethical and responsive decision-making. So while this book is 'Very Short', it is not a 'Very Simple How To ...' book about management because there are far too many of those around. It is designed to help managers, future managers and students of management to think more critically about what management is, who managers are and for what and whom are they responsible. In other words, it focuses on thinking about management differently: about the complexities, subtleties and uncertainties managers face.

## Why do we need different ways of thinking about managers and management?

Two main questions underpin each chapter: what might we be taking for granted when managing people and organizations? And given this, what ideas then strike us as being worth exploring because they encourage us to see things differently? We are going to examine aspects of management that are often taken for granted and treated as peripheral by other management books, yet which I believe are embedded within everyday management practice and integral to the effective management of people and organizations – relationships, encountering difference and acting ethically. These questions are important because managers and organizations play a pivotal role in the world today.

I wrote the first edition of the book in 2008, at a time when the news was full of the worldwide economic recession: the volatility of the FTSE and NYSE, the collapse and shoring up by governments of major financial institutions such as the Royal Bank of Scotland and big business corporations such as General Motors, as organizations were closing and laying off workers. Since then, numerous leadership and ethical scandals have rocked the world. Nearly every month there seems to be a new scandal: the News Corp hacking scandal in the UK, the New

Zealand Dotcom spying scandal, the Lehman Brothers scandal in the US, the worldwide Libor Fixing scandal, and so on. These are often attributed to unethical leadership, a corrupt culture and an unwillingness of managers to question unethical practices. In a 2013 speech, Simon Walker, the director general of the UK Institute of Directors, commented in relation to the Royal Bank of Scotland and Barclays scandal, that managers need to be held accountable after 'Shareholder value has been destroyed, capitalism has been given a bad name, key measures of the market have been manipulated for cynical gains, taxpayers have shelled out billions to bail banks out, and yet vast rewards packages are still being handed out'.[1] A focus purely on the bottom line can mean that the broader social responsibilities of management are ignored – an issue we'll address more explicitly in Chapter 5.

In recent years, management theorists and business schools have also come under criticism, notably for: focusing on the science and theory rather than the practice of management; encouraging students to learn business jargon and to replicate information rather than reflect critically on issues; and failing to address the moral responsibility of managers for crucial global issues such as poverty, sustainability and community development (Pfeffer and Fong, 2002; Poff, 2010). Khurana (2007) argues that business degrees are often designed around disciplines (finance, strategy, organizational behaviour, etc.) and narrow axiomatic research that leads to a focus on short-term gain. As a consequence, when students study topics in functional silos they graduate with a simplified understanding of management and a lack of knowledge of how the many different functions in organizations interrelate.

This all sounds quite damning! You may be wondering why bother doing a business studies degree or reading yet another book about management?! The crucial point is that *what managers do has an impact on people's lives*, on society at large and on the environment in which we live. And managers, like the rest of us, are human and fallible. Which surely means that the more ways managers have of viewing the world and exploring possibilities, the better able they will be to deal with uncertainty and complexity. This is why the ideas in this book draw on a 'critical' approach to management, which is designed to encourage you to think more critically and reflexively about the role and responsibilities of managers in organizations and in society at large.

The ideas are challenging, but nevertheless important in understanding the many issues and complexities facing managers today. Karl Weick, an American organizational theorist, emphasizes 'the generative properties of richness', that we need to have a 'head full of theories' (2007: 16) – to which I add 'ideas and questions' – if we want to be effective managers. In other words, we need to think in complicated ways if we want to understand complexity.

So I'll be offering a different lens for viewing management, managers and managing organizations. Rather than talking about management as techniques, generalized roles, or as a set of skills and competencies such as communicating, motivating and delegating, I will argue that managing is a relational, reflexive and moral practice: about who you are and how you relate to others. Because whether you are a production manager responsible for getting the product out the door, a nurse manager responsible for patient care, a school principal, or a research and development manager, you are not just managing work but you are also managing people. And people are not a coherent and malleable group of well-defined characteristics, clear intentions and predictable actions – as many mainstream management theories would have us believe.

Our experience tells us that people interpret the world and themselves differently; we have our own ideas about what's important and what needs to be done, and we like to do things our own way. We are naturally inquisitive, suspicious and emotional. We get scared, avoid issues and we rarely have all the answers. In other words, we are human and unique, and encounter others different from us on a moment-to-moment, day-to-day basis – in families, student groups, project management teams, meetings and in the pub. This is not, as conventional management theory states, just an issue of recognizing that we live in a 'network' or that 'stakeholders' have different interests, but understanding that each of us are unique individuals. So if we take this view, then how might we think of organizations and management? Certainly not in terms of organization structures and systems, nor as generalized management roles and functions.

Instead, I suggest that managing is about recognizing and respecting differences and relating to people in responsible and ethical ways, and that at the core of this is who you are as a person and how you relate to others. This requires thinking about managing and management from a more relational and reflexive stance: rethinking our relationship with the world around us and prodding taken-for-granted ways of doing things. We'll move away from realist views of the world, which underlie conventional organization and management theory, towards the idea that we have a dialectical relationship with our social world – we shape and are shaped by our experience as we talk and interact with others. So language is important: it's like breathing because we use it all the time, often without thinking about how our conversations work in subtle yet powerful ways to shape our surroundings and ourselves. The words we use in everyday conversations shape our sense of what 'the organization' is like, which influences what we do and say. However, I'll argue that bringing the crucial nature of language to the fore should not take us to impression management or managing meaning because these are yet other forms of persuasion and manipulation. Instead, it should take us to dialogue, which means recognizing that we shape meaning between us in relationally-responsive interaction.

## A critical approach to management

I was reminded of the importance of understanding the complexities of managing people and organizations back in 2008 when wandering through the Indian Pueblo Cultural Center in Albuquerque, New Mexico. I came across this story of emergence – the birth of the Native American people from the earth.

> *After we emerged,*
> *The world was flat and life*
> *was too easy.*
> *We soon forgot about our makers.*
> *So they created the mountains, mesas and valleys*
> *to make us humble*
> *and make us repentant.*
> *This is what our fathers tell us.*

> *Isleta Pueblo, Theodore Jojola*

As one of the oldest cultures in the USA, the Pueblo Indians have a rich and fascinating history, but one that is also a story of oppression, initially by the Spanish and then by the US Federal Government. It's a culture of survival and of difference. One of the most spectacular sites in New Mexico is that of the Acoma Pueblo, which sits on a 370 feet high sheer mesa nearly 6,500 feet above sea level. Acoma is an oral and a matriarchal society, with property being passed down to the youngest daughter in the family. When the Catholic Mission was built in the mid-1600s, under Spanish direction, Native American traditions and symbols were incorporated seemingly surreptitiously into the building – a form of symbolic resistance?[2] You cannot fail to connect with the different way of living at Acoma, adapted and preserved throughout the experience of being colonized.

I began with this story in the first edition of the book, and include it in this edition because I believe it offers an appropriate metaphor to describe the history and development of Management Studies. Most management theorizing over the last century – and indeed today – focuses on smoothing out organizational landscapes into nice, simple, cultivatable and manageable chunks. But as we will see, this can be problematic. The advent of Critical Management Studies (CMS) in the 1980s helped reveal the complexities of organizational landscapes and caused us to question the orderly management world we'd constructed and colonized: A world in which it became too easy to justify everything through the 'bottom line' – profit and shareholder value. This book is not about a flat world colonized by seemingly rational techniques that make management deceptively simple and managing supposedly easier. It is about the mountains, mesas and valleys, the hidden aspects of the management landscape, the features that might come into view when we start poking and prodding around into issues such as the nature of social and organizational realities, the importance of language, whether managers have any responsibilities beyond the bottom line, and the implications for managing organizations and people in ethical and moral ways.

This requires us to address some basic issues that philosophers have been struggling with for many years. We'll draw on the work of scholars such as Ferdinand de Saussure, Paul Ricoeur, Maurice Merleau-Ponty, Mikhail Bakhtin, Judith Butler and Joan Acker, linguists, philosophers and feminists who are concerned about the relationship of language, our world and ourselves. But before you yawn, close the book and put it back on the shelf, let me say that we'll discuss these issues from a very practical perspective, with the question of how they relate to managing organizations at the forefront. I am not a philosopher, but there are aspects of philosophy that fascinate me, particularly phenomenological, existential, hermeneutic and poststructuralist work, which grapple with questions such as:

- What is the nature of social reality?
- Who are we in the world?
- What does it mean to be an ethical person and act in moral ways?

These questions are interesting – not just from an intellectual perspective, but from a practical one – because they play into how we see ourselves and others, and how we live our lives with other people on an everyday and ongoing basis. They are also fundamental to managing organizations. Our beliefs about what managers should be doing are based on a primary set of assumptions about the way the world operates. But a good deal of management theorizing takes these assumptions for granted, and does not accept there are any alternative versions. In other words, the world is flat, uniform, unidimensional – and life is relatively easy. Management education also for the most part operates within this context and is part of the process of socializing people into becoming 'good' managers and 'good' organizational citizens – with a particular view of the world and definition of 'good' in mind.

Take, for example, the assumption underlying much of management theory today – that individuals are self-actualizing, operating in a social world that exists independently from them – versus the assumption that we are always in relation to other people and that we are continually shaping our social world in our everyday interactions. How might these assumptions affect how I view myself as a manager, how I do my job and the way I interact with employees? How might they influence what I see as 'good' knowledge and good practices in organizations? We'll be discussing these questions throughout the book.

I can't claim that understanding management from a philosophical perspective is a new idea. Indeed, going back to a 1960 *Harvard Business Review* article, 'Existentialism for the businessman', John Rice stated, 'All businessmen, whether or not we admit it, are philosophers in a sense. Philosophy provides a framework within which we interpret our experiences and judge ourselves and situations' (1960: 135). What struck me about this article was first that its author was a business person who presumably had taken the time to read some philosophy and write about it at a time it was not 'cool' to do so, and second that it was published in *Harvard Business Review* – a journal not noted for publishing philosophical articles, rather as a bastion of managerialism! So what happened to management in the intervening 50 years? The advent of Critical Management Studies in the 1980s and 1990s brought philosophy and critique to European and Australasian management schools, ideas still on the fringe of many North American business schools.

## Changes and chapter themes

This second edition is revised with the aim of making some pretty complex and challenging ideas even more accessible and relevant to readers. The reviewers of the first edition offered constructive feedback, much of which I have incorporated in this second edition. One major change from the first edition relates to splitting Chapter 1 into two, with the original Chapter 2 on language and the nature of reality placed in the middle because it sets up the main ideas for Chapter 3, which is now oriented around the various forms of identity-work in which managers engage. I have attempted to clarify the issues around being more critical and reflexive in terms of managing various taken-for-granted aspects of culture in Chapter 4. And Chapter 5 has been updated with current examples. In response to the reviewer's comments, I have included more international examples and studies. Finally, more up-to-date additional readings are listed.

A brief description of each chapter follows. The main theme of the book is:

> Managing is a relational, reflexive and ethical activity. It is not just something one *does*, but is more crucially *who one is* and *how we relate to others*.

This runs through all five chapters, which each cover a particular aspect of relational, reflexive and ethical managing.

Chapter 1 provides some basic definitions of management, examines the relationship between management theory and practice, offers a brief history of management as an academic discipline and practice, and outlines some conventional and mainstream theories of the role of a manager. The chapter then sets the context for the rest of the book by outlining the main elements of Critical Management Studies.

Chapter 2 addresses the assumptions about the nature of reality and language that underpin the notion of relational, reflexive and ethical managers. In particular, I question traditional models of language and communication and the idea that reality is independent from us, suggesting instead that we shape our social and organizational realities with others in our conversations. Language, dialogue and relationships are therefore a crucial and integral part of managing.

Chapter 3 takes a more 'critical' outlook on managing and who managers are, by suggesting that managing is about identity-work: that in carrying out their work, managers are also trying to shape their identity – a sense of who they are in relation to others. I then offer five different ways of thinking about managing from this perspective: one mainstream and four based on critical approaches.

Chapter 4 takes a critically-reflexive view on what is seen as an important element of any manager's job – that of managing culture. We examine the dark side of culture and why managers need to be aware of the silencing and marginalizing aspect of culture as a cult – a form of manipulation of hearts, minds and souls – that is so often taken for granted. I suggest that relational, reflexive and ethical managers need to view culture as a community of difference and to think about what that might mean.

Chapter 5 addresses what for me is *the* key concern of any manager – creating organizations that are just and moral and managing in ethical ways. We examine two main issues around the premise that managers have both a personal and an institutional responsibility to act in ethical ways: 1) that institutional codes of ethics alone are not enough to ensure people act in ethical ways; 2) that each of us takes responsibility for acting in ethical ways as well as ensuring that equity, morality and justice exist at an organizational level.

## Conclusion

So bear with me. The ideas in the book may be unfamiliar. They are about encountering difference and they are, I believe, crucially important to managers. To continue the emergence metaphor, you'll notice three paths weaving through the landscape that at some points separate and at others converge, but that always head in the same general direction – that how we relate to people and the world around us is the core of every aspect of management. The first path is about management as *relational*: the idea that we are always in relationship with others who are not the same as us. We therefore need to think about how we encounter difference, about the gendered and racialized nature of organizations and management, and how this relates to notions of identity, culture and organizing. The second path is about management as a *reflexive practice*: exploring the taken-for-granted relationship between language and our experience of the world, and examining the impact that assumptions of socially constructed realities have on management theory and practice. The third is about the *moral and ethical responsibility* of managers – not the normal path of business ethics, which focuses on codes of conduct, but how to *be* ethical in our relationships and interactions with others.

As you'll see, at the heart of the book is a fundamental questioning of who we are (as people and as managers) and how we experience organizational life and relate to other people. You may or may not agree with these ideas – I'm not claiming my way of viewing the world is the 'right' one – but I do believe that thinking through the issues and different ways of thinking about management, examining their practicality, assessing their possibilities and figuring out where you stand is important. And I've been encouraged over the years by the response of students, which often turns from cynicism, to interest, to engagement. You'll find comments from my conversations with managers and students throughout the book, to illustrate the ways in which they have connected the issues with their own experience as managers.

## Notes

1  www.iod.com/Influencing/Press-Office/press-releases/IoD-Director-General-speech-on-the-challenges-for-capitalism (accessed 4 September 2013).
2  See http://sccc.acomaskycity.org/visiting (accessed 5 September 2013).

# Management, Management Studies and Managerialism

This chapter begins with some basic definitions of management, examines the relationship between management theory and practice, offers a brief history of management as an academic discipline and practice, and then sets the context for the rest of the book by outlining the main elements of Critical Management Studies. This is important background information because not only does it help explain the way we understand management today, it also explains why management education and training programmes are designed the way they are and why managers do what they do. Management Studies has a long history going back to Frederick Taylor's (1911) work on Scientific Management, but over the last 20 years there have there been calls to critically interrogate these mainstream approaches to management, managing and management education by Critical Management Studies scholars.[1] We are going to take up the CMS challenge by looking at the various – often unproblematic – ways in which management and managers have been constructed over time, both in theory and in practice. We'll do so as a way of establishing the groundwork for one of the major premises of this book, that:

> Managing is a relational, reflexive and ethical activity. It is not just something one *does*, but is more crucially *who one is* and *how we relate to others*.

This means thinking more critically about the responsibilities of managers and engaging in debate about their place in society at large.

### Definitions

We'll begin with some brief definitions and then, because we are taking a critical perspective, go on to question the assumptions underlying these generally accepted definitions and look at alternative ways of thinking about management.

## Management

Management can be seen variously as a group of people managing an organization, a body of knowledge, skills and competencies, a social form, and a practice. First, managers as a group are differentiated from other groups such as professional, technical, scientific, manual and administrative employees. This differentiation occurs in linguistic and symbolic ways that play out in everyday interactions and conversations. Linguistically, written documents such as job descriptions, policy and procedure manuals outline the particular responsibilities and rights of management. We also talk about white-collar (management and professional), blue-collar (non-management and professional) employees, and direct reports (the employees reporting to a manager). These are not just symbolic forms of talk, the differences are also evident through dress, physical space and office décor, the type of technology, equipment and 'tools' used, parking spaces, and so on. Management is often a salaried group who receive rewards and fringe benefits that other employees do not. As a social form and practice: management is a recognizable career with responsibilities, rights and privileges considered as legitimate not only by organizational members, but also by members of society. Being part of 'management' carries a certain status within society, a position and career to which people aspire.

## Managers

The most common definition of managers is that they 'get things done and achieve organizational goals through other people'. In the first *Very Short ...* book, first published in 2006 and now in the third edition, Chris Grey (2013: 51–8) talks about the origins and interpretations of management: from the mundane meaning of managing to do something (I *managed* to get out of bed today), to the elitist view of management as a dominant social institution and an instrument of control. He outlines what it is that managers do when they manage: they solve problems, they control and discipline workers, they make things efficient, they might even make things more humane. They do so by representing and intervening: making activities and actions knowable by producing signs and texts (organization charts, job descriptions, product specifications, operational procedures, etc.), and then acting to make sure people and things do what they are supposed to be doing. Indeed, functionalist models of management – models based on the idea that it's the job of managers to achieve organizational goals through efficient structures and systems, and ordered behaviour – go back at least 60 years. These models also assume that people have to be socialized into behaving 'rationally' (i.e., goal-oriented) and carrying out their given roles within pre-existing structures and social realities.

Recently, research has grown around a different way of studying managers. Rather than focusing on generalized roles, management researchers now explore managerial identities: how managers shape their identity in their everyday activities. This approach assumes that as we go about living our life on a daily basis, we are trying to figure out who we are and what we should be doing: in other words, we are carrying out *identity-work*. Researchers working from this perspective explore how managers try to find some sort of connection between their personal and social identities and attempt to shape a relatively coherent sense of their identity (Watson, 2009). We'll explore the differences between these two approaches – models of managerial roles that focus on *what* managers do or should be doing, and studies of identity-work that focus on *how* managers create some sort of sense of who they are – in Chapter 3. I also want to note that the identity-work perspective underpins many of the ideas in this book … that managers are active in shaping themselves and their world.

## Management Studies

Management Studies is a body of knowledge, skills and competencies associated with managing organizations. It is based on research geared towards answering questions such as: 'What *is* management?', 'What do/should managers *do*?', and 'What skills and competencies do managers need?'. The resulting theories and models are seen as vital to the development of 'professional' managers, equipping them with the knowledge, techniques and skills necessary to manage organizations effectively and ultimately improve economic performance. Much of the work in Management Studies adopts a functionalist perspective, which aims to improve the efficiency and effectiveness of managers and their organizations by identifying the rational techniques and ways of behaving that promote this goal. From this perspective, the primacy of the bottom line – the maximization of profit – is axiomatic. As we will see, even critical perspectives (CMS) address these questions, although in a very different way.

## Critical Management Studies

Critical Management Studies scholars have argued that conventional ways of thinking about management are problematic because they often focus on simplified 'rational' and 'technical' versions of the world and ignore moral debates about the nature, purpose and impact of management and organizations. In particular, CMS critically examines the 'narrow instrumentality of work-process relationships' and presents other diverse 'interests and perspectives' (Alvesson and Willmott, 1992: 4–5). This means questioning what mainstream Management Studies takes for granted – the primacy of the profit motive and productivity and the legitimacy of management (the right to give orders and control others). The goal of CMS is to draw attention to the impact of a narrow functionalist way of thinking on people and society: who gets marginalized or hurt in the process and how managers and organizations can act in more socially and morally responsible ways.

CMS is based broadly on social constructionist ideas that our 'realities', identities and even knowledge itself are culturally, historically and linguistically situated, and shaped in the interaction between people. In other words, there isn't a social reality that exists independently from people. Critical scholars also argue that organizations are far from being 'neutral', they privilege certain groups of employees and 'stakeholders' over others. These assumptions form the basis for the central theme that management is a relational, reflexive and ethical practice. We will explore these ideas later in this chapter as well as in the chapters that follow.

## What is management theory and practice?

It's important to think about the relationship between theory and practice because the aim of management research and education is to influence practice. Theories provide the organizing themes for curriculum design, guidelines for course content, topics for teaching and models for management consulting and training. Think about management practices such as business process re-engineering, 360-degree feedback, performance measurement and talent management, all of which are heavily researched, taught in business schools and commonly used in organizations today. Yet despite this, the relationship between management theory and practice is seen to be problematic – usually by academics who believe that managers are not implementing the theories they've so carefully constructed!

The relevance of theory to practice came under scrutiny well over 30 years ago with criticisms that theory is divorced from practice and doesn't take into account the complexities and uncertainties managers face.[2] Management researchers have tried to narrow the theory–practice gap in a number of ways. Some study managers and their activities *inductively*, developing theory from practice by focusing on how people make sense of their experience. Inductive studies work from participant interpretations in particular contexts, for example, through the stories of managers themselves or by carrying out an ethnographic study in which the researcher spends an extended period of time in an organization observing activities and talking to employees (e.g., Kornberger, Justesen and Mouritsen, 2011; Reedy, 2009; Watson, 2001, 2011). Ian Palmer and Cynthia Hardy take a different approach in *Thinking about Management* (2000), where they aim to link academic management debates to practical management issues by organizing the debates around management activities such as: managing structure, managing people and managing power. Palmer and Hardy's book is *deductive*, still essentially theoretical with practical management-related exercises. Deductive studies of management apply or test general theories and/or hypotheses, for example by using large survey data.

Another way of narrowing the theory–practice gap lies through the co-production and co-consumption of knowledge. The *co-production* of knowledge involves academics and practitioners working together on the design, implementation and writing-up of research projects. While co-produced research can lead to more practice-relevant research, it is not without its challenges, as academic Kevin Orr and senior practitioner Mike Bennett (2012) discovered in their collaborative study of UK public sector leadership. They found themselves negotiating the politics of co-production: the different demands, expectations and values of their institutions and professions, and different ideas about the purpose of research and how it should be carried out. Heusinkveld, Sturdy and Werr (2011) address the issue from the angle of *co-consumption*, arguing that in addition to thinking about how knowledge is produced, we also need to think about how it's consumed or used in practice. Consumers of management knowledge are not passive, but they adapt, develop and re-create knowledge and techniques as they implement them. So why don't academics work with managers and study how knowledge emerges in the implementation of their theories?

A growing field of research that explicitly addresses the theory–practice gap is that of *practice-based studies* (PBS), which focus on the 'real work' that is done in organizations. Organizational sociologist Silvia Gherardi (2009), influential in PBS, differentiates between studying practice from:

a) The outside, where researchers look for regularities and patterns associated with specific practices. For example, studies of strategy that examine how managers 'do' or 'make' strategy – known as the strategy-as-practice approach (see the 2008 VSFI book on strategy by Carter, Clegg and Kornberger for an overview and critique, and also Whittington, 2006).

b) The inside, from the point of view of the people engaged in the practice. Researchers working from this perspective are interested in *situated action* and *communities of practice*: how people together make sense of what's going on, learn and generate knowledge by forging 'relations and connections among all the resources available and the constraints present' (Gherardi, 2009: 117). For example, Davide Nicolini (2011) carried out a practice-based ethnographic study of telemedicine (caring for patients at a distance) at three hospitals in Italy. He not only observed and talked with managers and staff, but asked practitioners to comment on the results of his research.

Practice-based studies focus not just on what people do, but also what they know, and how that knowing both influences and is influenced by practice.

Finally, I want to draw your attention to a more critical way of thinking about the relationship between theory and practice. In a study of the dissemination of management knowledge in Finland, Kantola and Seeck (2011) found that Harvard Business School Professor Michael Porter's well-known ideas on national competitiveness were used to change the direction of Finnish industrial policies: reflecting a culture of *consultocracy* (Hood and Jackson, 1991) in which academics and business consultants advise government on policy issues. Kantola and Seeck argue, controversially, this is a form of state-initiated social engineering, because packaged management theories based on economic principles were used to legitimate politicians' actions in changing social policy, especially in relation to welfare cuts. They also claim that this is counter to the democratic government ideals of civic participation and debate, because management knowledge often advocates the implementation of one best practice rather than a plurality of viewpoints. This example is important because it highlights the broader social and ethical issues that can arise when theories are applied to practice in uncritical ways. It also raises the need for managers and academics to be *reflexive* – to think about what they are taking for granted – and *relational* – by thinking about who is affected by their actions/theories, and what their moral responsibilities are. As I write (February 2013), the UK Royal Bank of Scotland, which is over 80 per cent taxpayer owned, is again being criticized because they are reporting losses of £5 billion while paying out £607 million in bonuses.

To summarize, management theory and practice are interwoven in many ways, not just in terms of the application of theory to practice, but also in the co-production of knowledge and in practice-based studies. If we begin to take a critical approach by asking 'what are we are taking for granted?', then new ways of thinking about the theory–practice relationship emerge – for example, how managers re-shape knowledge as they 'consume' it, and how management theories and techniques are used unthinkingly in contexts where they are not entirely appropriate and have unanticipated consequences that affect the well-being of employees and society at large.

## Management and managerialism

### Before we start …

Let's begin this journey through the development of Management Studies with three 'critical' thoughts in mind:

1. That management is *ethnocentric* – the history of management is based mainly on work done in the USA (and secondarily in Europe) and consequently westernized cultural values and ways of managing are seen to be superior to any other. Management education draws mainly on research done in western organizations, studies within eastern cultures often conform to American ways of doing research and theorizing, and there are few studies from the south. We will address this later when we look at the branch of CMS known as postcolonialism.

2. That management is *gendered* – a *his*tory mainly written by men, about men and for men. This may seem to be a controversial statement, but when I started teaching in a UK business school over 25 years ago, there were only two female management faculty members and we often taught management courses with no female students. Before the 1970s there were few female management or organization theory authors (Mary Parker Follett, Rosabeth Kanter and Rosemary Stewart being exceptions). This often goes unnoticed and is still the case today. A few years ago I proposed an all-female symposium at the Academy of Management conference, in response to sitting through four all-male symposia the previous year. One reviewer asked why we thought a group of female postmodern academics represented the diversity of organization theory – a question I'm sure that was not asked of the all-male symposia participants?!

So management was and, as we will see in Chapter 4, still largely is *man*agement, not just in terms of the number of male versus female managers, but also in relation to the gendered nature of organizational practice.

3. That we are studying the *Discourse* of management. You may be unfamiliar with this term, especially if you haven't come across Critical Management Studies before. A number of CMS scholars draw on French philosopher Michel Foucault's (1972) idea of Discourse as a body of knowledge and system of thought that has developed over time and is 'acknowledged to be truthful, involving exact description, well founded reasoning, or necessary presupposition' (1972: 57). Foucault writes that each Discourse contains 'rules' which are unconsciously used by scientists to maintain the unity of their discipline and to give their work credibility: 'to define the objects proper to their own study, to form their concepts, to build their theories' (Foucault, 1970: xi). These rules drive research and theory in a Discourse because they provide a focus and a modus operandi for study – and an ideology. We will see an example of this when we look at the 'rules' that constitute the ideology of managerialism, rules based on the functionalist Discourse I outlined above (p. 2–3). Discourses of management are therefore organized, theoretical and ideological forms of studying and talking about management and organizations.

## The history of management studies

The emergence of management in this [twentieth] century may have been a pivotal event of history. It signaled a major transformation of society into a pluralist society of institutions, of which managements are the effective organs. (Peter F. Drucker, 1973: 1)

As Peter Drucker states in the quote above, management is the organ or instrument enabling an institution to function. Managers do so by ensuring the institution achieves its mission; producing economic results; making work and workers productive; and by 'managing social impacts and social responsibilities' (1973: 40). The latter refers not just to providing jobs, but also to the impact of organizations on local, national and global economies, on the physical and social environment, and on the well-being of people. In this way, management is central to modern society. But how did it become so? Figure 1.1 offers one way of making sense of how management has developed as a topic of study and an important social practice over the last century.

**Academic Lens**

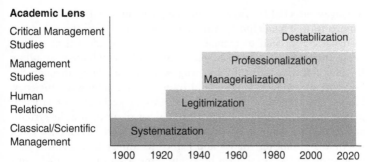

**Figure 1.1**   A brief history of management

I've identified four distinct but overlapping phases, associated with developments in management research, theory and practice. The 'academic lens' axis relates to the major theoretical Discourses of management. Each phase highlights the impact of that Discourse on management research, education and practice.

### In the beginning: systematization …

In the early twentieth century, Management and Organization Studies did not exist as a formal discipline or practice. There was no recognizable body of knowledge or a profession known as management. A number of academics and practitioners began the search for the best way of managing and designing organizations, which they believed could be achieved by developing more 'scientific' and systematic approaches to managing organizations. Their work is collectively known as the Classical and Scientific Management schools of thought, which formed the prehistory of Management Studies and played a major role in the systematization, legitimization and professionalization of the field. The impact of Classical and Scientific Management is still felt today in business school curricula and in management practice. Time and motion studies, the 'scientific' measurement and control of work and evidenced-based management all draw on this legacy. Because this book is about management rather than organization studies in general, I'm going to focus on a few key figures in the field of Management Studies.[3]

We can begin the story of the systematization and legitimization of management with Frederick Taylor's book *The Principles of Scientific*

*Management* (1911). Taylor, chief engineer at the Bethlehem Steel Company in Philadelphia, was concerned with developing a more systematic approach to management through the identification and application of scientific principles that would simultaneously allow the maximization of profit and wage-earning capability through the lowering of production costs and by increasing employee efficiency. He set out a number of principles he saw as necessary for efficient management, including the scientific analysis of work and the systematic hiring and training of employees. Taylor's work became the basis for time and motion studies and helped legitimize management as a profession and a social form by establishing a set of 'scientific' management practices.

Yet his work was not without its critics, most notably in relation to the deskilling (Braverman, 1974) and dehumanization of the work environment that resulted from breaking work down into unskilled, standardized and highly repetitive tasks. One need only watch the first ten minutes of Charlie Chaplin's satirical 1936 film *Modern Times*, notably the automated feeding machine designed to feed workers while they worked, to grasp the effect of the Taylor system on the well-being and the morale of employees. The film also highlights Fordism, a system of production named after American industrialist Henry Ford, who adopted Scientific Management principles in his automotive manufacturing business in the 1920s. Fordism incorporates Taylor's ideas with the mass production of goods through an assembly-line process.

The impact of systematization was that it formalized the role and the power of managers by creating the reason why managers should exist and established their right to give orders, along with the techniques and principles that set them apart from other employees.

### ... Followed by legitimization ...

Legitimacy is the credibility given to an organization or person based on their ability to conform and support social norms, values and expectations (Powell and DiMaggio, 1983). Legitimization is the process by which credibility is earned, given and/or perceived to be acceptable by others. In addition to Taylor, Mary Parker Follett, Henri Fayol, Luther Gulick and Chester Barnard also wrote influential books. Mary Parker Follett was a pioneering American scholar and management consultant who, back in 1918, examined the nature of power, advocated individual and community development, and democratic forms of organization, including self-governing groups. Her radical (for the time) interest in social consciousness, participative decision-making and in developing community-based rather than hierarchical structures was echoed later by Chester Barnard, president of the New Jersey Bell Telephone Company. In his 1938 book, *The Functions of the Executive*, Barnard argued that managers needed to create cooperative organizational systems in which work should be integrated by establishing and communicating goals and motivating workers to achieve the goals.

Contrast Follett's ideas with those of Henri Fayol, CEO of a French mining company, whose work is explicitly and implicitly concerned with establishing the right of managers to manage. In his 1916 book, *General and Industrial Management* (1949), Fayol specified five functions of management (planning, organizing, commanding, coordinating and controlling), along with 14 principles of administration, which included the unity-of-command (each subordinate reporting only to one boss) and the scalar principle, where all organizational members are to be controlled by being placed in a hierarchical structure resembling a pyramid. Gulick, a Professor of Municipal Science and Administration at Columbia University in the 1930s, and Urwick, a British management consultant, built on Fayol's work by devising the famous mnemonic POSDCoRB (**P**lanning, **O**rganizing, **S**taffing, **D**irecting, **Co**ordinating, **R**eporting and **B**udgeting) to describe the functions of a chief executive. This work (1937) had a major impact on management in public sector and government organizations, primarily in the USA, but also in the UK.

It's interesting to note that while Taylor's, Fayol's, Barnard's and Gulick and Urwick's work essentially accepted and reinforced a manager's right to manage, Follett's (1924) ground-breaking work emphasized the more humanistic role of managers and their broader social responsibilities through her notion of *power-with* rather than power-over: the joint development of power based on interactive influence between community members and between organizational members. She argued that while the development of power-with takes time, it is nevertheless important because it is a true reflection of the democratic ideals of society that lead to personal and social development.

The Human Relations School, which began with the Hawthorne Studies in the 1920s, shifted the focus to the need for managers to consider people and the social factors at play in work. While the studies began by examining the impact of the work environment on productivity, the researchers discovered that issues such as consultation, informal group processes and the motivation of workers were influential factors in worker productivity. While the Hawthorne Studies are criticized in terms of their experimental validity, they nevertheless offered an important turning point in management and are regarded as the foundation of the discipline of organizational behaviour by focusing attention on individual and group behaviour, motivation, leadership and communications. It is also worth noting that (from a CMS perspective) while this concern for people and the humanization of management is ostensibly altruistic, at its heart lies a concern for improving productivity by controlling the behaviour of employees.

If we go back to Chris Grey's idea that management is a process of representation and intervention, then we can see this occurring in these first two phases of management. Systematization is about trying to make management knowable by naming and re-presenting activities, behaviours and responsibilities, and by establishing a bag of management tools that can be used to manage organizations efficiently and effectively. By creating this formal body of expertise based on 'scientific' principles and activities, management becomes more credible and managers more authoritative because they have legitimate intervention techniques to control people, direct their activities and make changes. I suggest systematization and legitimization are also about difference and distance. By creating specialized knowledge, management becomes different and separate from other professions, jobs and work activities. And difference and distance are seen as essential to maintaining control – as Taylor argued, managers should manage and workers do the work.

### Managerialization

*Managerialization* is often associated with the rise of the managerial class and of a managerialist ideology. Peter Drucker (1973) saw the period between World War II and the 1960s as a management boom that changed society permanently because management became a familiar term, a legitimate social practice and a position of status supported by institutional and social norms that gave managers the right to hire, fire, give orders, control and evaluate the performance of others in the interest of efficiency, productivity, profit or providing a service for the common good.[4] Chris Grey suggests that consequently management became the 'bulwark of civilization', yet also ironically a 'perennially failing operation' because organizational and managerial problems continue to demand new and improved techniques and approaches. This failure has led to the growth of Human Resource Management, Management and Organization Studies, management consultants and the emergence of management gurus such as W. Edwards Deming and Tom Peters.

Along with the management boom came managerialism which, as Stan Deetz (1992) argues in *Democracy in an Age of Corporate Colonization*, is 'a kind of systemic logic, a set of routine practices, and an ideology ... a way of doing and being' (1992: 222) in organizations which has the ultimate goal of enhancing efficiency through control. But what does this mean and how does ideology relate to management practice?

An *ideology* is a system of beliefs, values, ideas, interests, social structures and practices that explicitly and implicitly shape the way we see and make sense of our experience. This system inevitably has an underlying logic that also influences the way we do things and how we evaluate what is good or bad, appropriate or inappropriate action. Capitalism is a prime example – the belief that organizations have to be managed for the economic benefit of owners. The American Dream, the German Protestant Work Ethic, and Swedish egalitarianism are also ideologies that play through our organizational lives in formal ways, for example, through promotion criteria and the provision of personal development activities. The American Dream, the belief that we can gain material wealth, success, happiness and be who we want to be if we work hard and strive to achieve, has practical consequences for the ways in which US organizations are managed and employees are evaluated and promoted. US organizational culture often values individualism, competitiveness, risk taking, assertiveness and 'doing what it takes' to get short-term results: values that Geert Hofstede (1985, 2001) claimed were typically American. Based on a study of the IBM Corporation in different countries, he suggested that management styles, policies and practices are influenced by the cultural values in each country. For example, in Latin America group commitment is highly valued, in Sweden work–life balance is important and in China the focus is on the long term, whereas in the UK and US individualism and short-term results are more important. Hofstede also concluded that the way managers are perceived varies: in the US managers are cultural heroes and sell their skills where they can, compared to Germany where engineers are the cultural heroes and managers must work their way up the ranks.

A *managerialist ideology* addresses the role, responsibilities and rights of managers in a capitalist society. This includes the beliefs that:

Managers are the instruments and administrators of capitalism, and act in line with the common good.

Managers are skilled experts who have the right to act as agents for owners and shareholders.

Managerial work is characterized by rationality and neutrality.

Managers pursue efficiency by minimizing costs and maximizing profit and productivity.

Managers have the right to make decisions and give instructions to employees without seeking their consent.

Managers use rational, analytical and scientific management techniques to resolve problems and increase efficiency and productivity. For example, through Total Quality Management (TQM), Business Process Improvement (BPI), and Performance Management.

**Figure 1.2**   Managerialism

These beliefs and practices are regarded as *old managerialism*, in contrast to new forms of managerialism, which seem to have taken on a life of their own in government services, education, health care and other public sector organizations throughout Europe, Australasia and North America. *New managerialism* includes 'emphasizing the primacy of management above all other activities; monitoring employee performance (and encouraging self-monitoring too); the attainment of financial and other targets ...' (Deem and Brehony, 2005: 220) and has extended into the public sector through *new public management* where it is associated with importing a market orientation and business practices as a means of maximizing organizational performance, service and profit. This includes cost-cutting measures, increased regulation, the privatization of services, re-engineering and evidence-based management. Jeffrey Pfeffer and Robert Sutton (2006) argue that evidence-based management means making decisions and acting on 'hard facts', which involves: demanding evidence; examining the logic underlying the evidence and any faulty cause-and-effect reasoning; encouraging experimentation to test viability; and reinforcing continuous learning.

Both old and new managerialism are ideological, authoritative and viewed by CMS scholars as being oppressive – an issue we will take up in the section on destabilization, where we will find managerialism under attack. This view is not just confined to academics – in a 2012 article in Britain's *Telegraph* newspaper, Charles Moore argued that managerialism results in bloodless bean-counters, social division, and uses a managerialist language based partly on 'semi-spiritual banality', for example, 'unlocking energies'![5]

## ... Along with professionalization

Recall that Foucault (1970) claimed that Discourse and knowledge are powerful because they impact the purpose and practices of institutions. Management Discourse legitimates the work of business schools, and the qualifications offered by business schools legitimate management as a profession.

The Scientific Management, Classical and Human Relations Schools formed the groundwork for legitimizing management as a field of study and as a profession, by developing a body of knowledge and expertise around the management of organizations. This body of knowledge provided a basis for establishing formal management qualifications, a system of practice, and professional bodies to regulate and oversee entry, evaluation and promotion to the profession. The first business school still in existence today, the *École Supérieure de Commerce de Paris* was founded in France 1819,[6] and the first MBA was offered by Harvard Business School in 1910. In 1923 the American Management Association was established, followed by the British Institute of Management in 1947. However, it was the 1960s and 1970s that saw a growth of Management and Organization Studies and the more widespread emergence of business schools. Business degrees continued to gain popularity in the 1980s and 1990s[7] across Europe, Asia, Australasia and North America.

From the 1960s onwards, management training also took a hold with the growth of in-company training and development courses and external training and consulting organizations. In the 1990s, corporate universities became popular in US companies such as Motorola, McDonalds and Disney, providing management, leadership, quality and operations training. These developments not only professionalized management, but also established it as a social form and a sought-after career. I began my career in the 1970s working in management training in the gas industry and the National Health Service. We ran numerous courses on the principles of supervision, foundations of management, advanced courses on management and various management topics such as hiring, firing, communicating, motivating and planning. We hired academics to contribute to these courses because they brought a sense of legitimacy to the material. I moved into education, where I taught courses leading to certificates, diplomas, undergraduate and postgraduate degrees in management. These courses, still today, draw on a number of empirical studies of management defining the characteristics of managerial work, managerial functions, roles and/or competencies.[8]

There have been many journal articles and a plethora of books, both academic and practitioner-oriented, on the nature of managerial work. But five authors have been particularly influential in contributing to the professionalization of management: Sune Carlson's (1951) study of Swedish executives, Rosemary Stewart's (1967, 1976, 1982) work on UK managers, Henry Mintzberg's (1973) study of CEOs, and John Kotter's (1982) and Richard Boyatzis's (1982) studies of US managers. Their work is notable because it was empirical, examining the work activities and behaviour of managers, using a variety of methods including work diaries, interviews, observation, an analysis of contacts and communications, job performance analysis and testing. Their main findings are summarized in Table 1.1.

What they found contradicted the classical view of management as a rational, ordered and unambiguous practice as advocated by Fayol, Gulick and Taylor. Instead, these studies suggest that managerial work is ill-defined, uncertain and fragmented. Consequently, managers and executives are subject to many pressures and find themselves: making choices within constraints, communicating and building networks in order to get things done, and often reacting to situations rather than having time to plan and organize. It's also important to note that underlying much of this work lie functionalist and *realist* assumptions that there is an external reality; that organizations exist as structures and systems; that norms and principles govern human behaviour; and that we can identify a set of universal managerial characteristics, roles and competencies that can be generalized across organizations and managers. We'll address these underlying assumptions in more depth in Chapters 2 and 3. Just note here that they result in generalized and prescriptive models of managerial roles, work and activities, used to educate and train managers to be more effective. These models helped form the basis for establishing management as a profession with a distinct body of knowledge and expertise.

| Sune Carlson (1951) | Rosemary Stewart (1967) | Henry Mintzberg (1973) | John Kotter (1982) | Richard Boyatzis (1982) |
|---|---|---|---|---|
| *Executive work* | *Managerial work* | *Managerial roles* | *Context, responsibilities and emergent demands* | *Management competencies* |
| Studied the characteristics of executive work | Studied how managers spend their time | Studied what managers do | Studied the behaviour of general managers | Characteristics leading to managerial effectiveness |
| CEOs deviate from efficient behaviour (pathologies) <br> Geography and a CEO's use of space are important | *Activities:* <br> • Liaising and establishing contacts <br> • Maintaining work <br> • Innovating and risk taking <br> • Setting job boundaries | *Interpersonal roles:* <br> • Figurehead <br> • Leader <br> • Liaison <br><br> *Informational roles:* <br> • Monitor <br> • Disseminator <br> • Spokesperson | *Emergent demands:* <br> • Setting goals, policies, etc. <br> • Achieving a delicate balance in allocating resources <br> • Keeping on top of complex activities <br> • Making decisions in uncertainty | • Efficiency orientation: goal and achievement oriented <br> • Concern with impact: power and influence <br> • Proactive: self-driven <br> • Self-confidence: decisive <br> • Oral presentation skills <br> • Conceptualization: inductive reasoning <br> • Deductive reasoning |
| *Pathologies:* <br> • Wishful thinking <br> • Becoming slaves to their diary <br> • Lack of time for undisturbed work <br> • Too heavy a workload <br> • Inefficient use of committees <br> • Unwillingness to establish policies | *Context:* <br> • Demands: what managers must do <br> • Constraints: factors limiting activities <br> • Choices: opportunities for individual managers to perform differently | *Decisional roles:* <br> • Entrepreneur <br> • Disturbance handler <br> • Resource allocator <br> • Negotiator | • Getting information, cooperation and support from bosses etc. <br> • Motivating and controlling a diverse group <br> • Implementation of work | • Uses socialized power: networks, mobilizes people <br> • Manages group processes: encourages teamwork |
| *Key issue: identifies the pathologies of executive behaviour* | *Key issue: highlights variety and situational influences in managerial work* | *Key issue: focuses on roles as ideal sets of behaviours* | *Key issue: need to develop flexible agendas and networks* | *Key issue: identifies competencies as a basis for training.* |

It's interesting to note that the managerialization and profession-alization of Management Studies continued to gain currency – and indeed increase in value – in the US during the 1990s and the new millennium. Most US business school curricula continue to centre on the techniques, processes and systems required to increase productiv-ity and efficiency and based on training managers and aspiring man-agers to become professional 'master' managers. This is interesting because during this period of certainty and confidence in capitalism and managerialism in the US, an element of doubt began to creep into European-based Management Studies as we began recognize that management as both a practice and a body of knowledge is *performa-tive*: constructed and maintained in interaction and conversation through discursive norms and practices. As such it is therefore contest-able. We'll look at performativity in more depth in Chapter 3, for the moment I want to raise two contested issues:

1. Is management a profession?
2. Should managers and managerialism benefit the greater social good or just shareholders?

A profession is defined as having the following characteristics: a definable body of knowledge, education programmes that incorporate formal examinations, a professional association, members have control over their work, and a formal code of ethics (Wilensky, 1964). Richard Barker (2010) argues management is *not* a profession because you are not required to have an MBA to be a manager, and MBA programmes don't prepare students to be managers in the same way as medical or law pro-grammes. And while there are various professional management associa-tions such as the British and Australian Institutes of Management, which have codes of conduct, these are only guidelines. Managers do not have a Hippocratic Oath or a General Medical Council to supervise their con-duct as in the medical profession.

In his 2007 book, *From Higher Aims to Hired Hands*, Rakesh Khurana also questions whether management is a profession – and links this to the issue of whether managers should be concerned only with efficiency and profit. He argues that investor capitalism in the 1980s and 1990s, along with the growth of MBAs and of models of management helped shift the perception of managers as caretaking bureaucrats to 'swashbuckling, iconoclastic champion(s) of "share-holder value"' (2007: 3). In doing so, this established both the legiti-macy and moral bankruptcy of management – an issue we will address further in Chapter 5. So there have been criticisms of conventional models that take for granted a manager's right to act solely in accordance with 'the bottom line'. The financial crisis of 2007–2008 and the many scandals since then have led to a questioning of financial and management practices and the weaknesses in corporate governance (see, for example, Kirkpatrick, 2009).

You might find these issues troubling – especially if you are doing a degree in Business Studies or Management with the goal of becoming a 'professional' manager! But if you are reading this book, it's probably because your professor believes that taking a critical perspective and exploring alternative views on the nature and role of management is important in becoming a responsible and ethical manager. Education is not only about preparing us to be good managers (as managerialism would have us believe), but is also about questioning what seems 'normal', what it means to be a good citizen/manager, and from whose point of view. It also means thinking beyond management theories and techniques to question the very purpose of management and the role of organizations in the world. That is, thinking about thinking differently, which German philosopher Martin Heidegger urges us to do in *Discourse on Thinking* (1966). He differentiates between calculative thinking and meditative thinking. Calculative thinking is typical of Scientific Management and of professionalization: getting the facts, analysing, categorizing things and people and making rational decisions. He sees calculative thinking as *willing*, that we *will* something into being a 'reality' and fix it as a truth because we think about it as real. For example, we talk about systems in organizations as if they exist independently from us. Meditative thinking is about being thoughtful and open to hidden meanings, to what 'at first sight doesn't go together at all' (Heidegger, 1966: 53), rather than trying to define, fix meanings and come to solutions quickly. This means feeling comfortable with uncertainty, debating and critiquing different interpretations and imagining new possibilities ... Which is the purpose of this book because meditative thinking can be linked to reflexivity.

We didn't really think about critique and hidden meanings until we started to draw on ideas from outside Management Studies from the late 1980s onwards. We realized there were some interesting conversations occurring in sociology, cultural anthropology, linguistics and philosophy that raised key questions about what we were doing in our research and teaching as management academics. The issues these questions raised also had implications for management practice. And so the late 1980s and 1990s saw the birth of Critical Management Studies in Europe and the destabilization of Management Studies.

### And so to destabilization … more about critical management studies

Critical Management Studies scholars draw from critical theory, postmodern and poststructuralist theory, critical sociology, philosophy and linguistics, to unpack and offer alternative understandings of management. Indeed, the very first *Very Short …* book is part of this destabilization process because its purpose was to communicate a critical perspective on organization theory in a more reader-friendly way.[9] While there is a common misconception that CMS means criticizing everything, this is not the case. It is about making the familiar strange and thinking about management differently as a means of opening up possibilities for developing more responsive, creative and ethical ways of managing organizations. While CMS addresses a range of issues, concerns and approaches, I suggest there are three main underlying themes of particular relevance to managers and students of management:

- Reality is not what you think it is: the crisis of representation, the constructed nature of managing and organizing (relationality).
- Everything is political: critiquing the political nature of management and ideological ways of thinking and acting (reflexivity).
- Suspicion is on the rise: questioning what we take for granted and developing reflexive, relational and ethical approaches to managing.

### Reality is not what you think it is

In our brief history of management we've seen that over the last century, management theory was (and often still is) about making management more rational, scientific and systematic by providing a set of management theories, models, principles and techniques – usually underpinned by a functionalist perspective based on the idea that there's a real structured world out there that exists independently from us (a *realist* ontology). Yet, as we will see, this notion of an objective reality is up for grabs. Cultural anthropologists and sociologists such as James Clifford (1983), George Marcus (with Fischer, 1986), Harold Garfinkel (1967) and Clifford Geertz (1983) questioned our relationship with our social world and the ways in which we account for our experience. They were particularly concerned with asking whether 'real' social realities and identities exist separately from our experience of those realities; whether we all experience realities in the same way; and whether we are able to explain – *represent* – social realities in neutral and accurate ways. They argued that social realities are constructed and shaped as we interact with each other and try to make sense of what is going on around us. This brings us to the idea that society and organizations are not pre-existing 'structures', but continually emerging in ongoing interactions and dialogue. Organizational members (managers and employees) are therefore co-constructors of their organizational realities – whether or not they realize it. This is an idea we will explore further in this and the following chapters.

Knowledge is not immune from this process. Our theories and 'facts' about the world are also socially constructed, and just as managers have their own situated and contextualized ways of making sense, so do academics. The models of managerial work we've seen in Table 1.1 are not about what managers *really* do, but are a *researcher's constructions* of what she or he thinks that managers are doing. And there's a performative issue here, because the so-called objective, simplified academic model is often viewed as the reality – what managers do and should be doing. Our perception of management and organizational practices are filtered through, and reinforce, these models because we seek patterns of behaviour that fit the categories identified in the model. Even more importantly, evaluations are made about a manager's effectiveness based on whether she or he fits the model, performs the role correctly or has the prescribed competencies.

CMS scholars are interested in destabilizing and exploring theories and categorizations, looking for alternative conceptualizations and practices and examining the potential consequences for managing people and organizations. They ask: *What is being taken for granted here? If we accept that we socially construct our world with others in our everyday interactions, then what responsibility does this bring?*

### Everything is political

One branch of CMS lies within poststructuralism, where scholars use a Foucauldian perspective to argue that realities and subjectivities are constructed both by discursive practices (linguistic systems and ways of talking, texts, ways of thinking, etc.) and non-discursive practices (institutional structures, social practices, techniques, etc.). As we saw earlier (p. 8) these discursive and non-discursive practices regulate what we accept as 'normal' and what we do not. We are often unaware of this normalizing process because we are products of it – it's only when we move into a different context, for example another organization, or if a new colleague starts to question us, that we realize what it is that we are taking for granted. If you connect our previous discussion of Foucault's notion of Discourse with the history of Management Studies, you may see that Discourses are powerful. They not only determine what is seen to be 'good' knowledge, they also influence the purpose and operation of institutions; what are counted as 'good' standards for judgement; and who are viewed as experts. Everything is political because all of these privilege particular ideologies, social structures, institutional practices and groups (Foucault, 1970, 1972), which ultimately influence who controls meaning and can speak for others. The Foucauldian branch of CMS examines power relationships and forms of control and discipline within organizational settings and relationships.

A second branch of CMS is based on Marxist and neo-Marxist analyses of the politics of capitalism, organization and work. Within this branch of work, critical theorists and labour process theorists examine the various forms of control that privilege elite groups of owners, shareholders and managers, and lead to the domination of other groups. One of the issues studied by critical theorists is why workers willingly consent to their own exploitation and accept this exploitation as 'normal', and how, on the other hand, they might resist this exploitation. Labour process theorists argue that managers control workers by systematically de-skilling work so that workers can be easily replaced. We'll explore these aspects of power further in Chapter 4.

CMS also destabilizes the ideologies of managerialism and new managerialism by asking us to think about them in different ways (e.g., Currie, McElwee and Somerville, 2012). While managerialism is claimed to be about the common good (see Figure 1.1), profit and shareholder value often drive decision-making to the detriment of the common good. Two recent examples include the Bangladesh factory collapse of April 2013 and the 2011 Envio recycling company toxic pollution case in Germany. At least 370 garment workers died when a Bangladesh factory collapsed. Cracks were found in the building the day before the collapse, but workers were forced to return to work by factory managers concerned about meeting production schedules. Envio employees dismantling industrial capacitators were found to have cancer-inducing PCB toxins far exceeding standard levels.

New managerialism, which as we have seen centres on techniques such as evidence-based management, has also come under critique. Mark Learmonth and Nancy Harding (2006), for example, argue that what constitutes 'evidence' is contested. Evidence-based management constructs what are seen to be neutral facts and data in a particular way, thus privileging 'scientific' evidence over other forms such as experiential knowledge. This in turn perpetuates the domination of some groups (managers) in the organization over others. They are not suggesting we throw evidence out, but that we broaden and take a more pluralistic view of what we consider to be evidence.

A number of CMS scholars focus on the role that business schools play in perpetuating a managerialist ideology. Some have suggested that MBA programmes are market-driven commodities in which faculty are producers and students are consumers needing to be satisfied, and that we need a critical pedagogy of practice in which students question taken-for-granted practices, reconstruct themselves as managers and rethink the purpose of their organizations (Welsh and Dehler, 2007).

*Postcolonialism* is a third branch of CMS that draws from cultural studies. It is of particular interest because of the globalization of business and the increasing influence of multinational corporations. I mentioned earlier that we often take for granted that Management Studies is westernized and ethnocentric. For example, we teach westernized management techniques and practices to multicultural classes with international students. Such techniques can be tools of colonialism, an imposition of culture and an exploitation of the people, material and economic resources of the colonized country. Postcolonialist scholars, particularly Edward Said (1993) and Homi Bhabha (1994), argued that this privileges the colonizer's culture because it is assumed to be more civilized, the right worldview, the right rationality, set of values, way of behaving, etc. This is usually to the detriment of other cultural values and experiences, alternative forms of knowledge and other voices. This really struck me when living and teaching in New Mexico, USA, which has a strong Native American culture. Native American views of leadership are very different from westernized views because they focus on relationships and responsibility for the community and the land,[10] values also prevalent in African leadership (Nkomo, 2011). Yet we teach westernized leadership theories without regard for different cultures and approaches. Studies of indigenous leadership are extremely rare: Kenny and Fraser's (2012) book on indigenous leadership in Canada, the USA and New Zealand is one exception.

This has obvious implications for managing global organizations because, postcolonialists argue, powerful multinational corporations have spearheaded the homogenization of different cultures into one westernized global culture that has disenfranchised and impoverished many people. This assimilation of different cultures has become known as the McDonaldization or Disneyfication of culture.[11] The impact of this assimilation is potently illustrated in Jack et al.'s (2011) scenario of a woman in India, Lakshmi, who works in a Bangalorean call centre, where she immediately becomes 'Carol', reminding UK and US customers to pay their bills. This highlights the invasiveness of westernized thinking not just in conforming to western work practices but also to western identities, which are privileged in that they are assumed to be 'better' than eastern identities.

Postcolonial organization theorists call for a plurality of cultural values, perspectives, narratives and identities (e.g., Thadhani, 2005) and knowledge about management and organizations that is not only co-produced by researchers from different cultures, but those researchers acknowledge the potentially colonializing impact of their own historical and cultural context (Özkazanç-Pan, 2008) – a postcolonial reflexivity (Spivak, 1999).

## Suspicion is on the rise

A third CMS critique argues that much of Management Studies to date is not only managerialistic, thereby privileging the few, but is also reductionist in the sense of trying to simplify a complex, ideological, political and social process to a set of principles, roles and techniques justified by one supposed rationality. This knowledge is packaged for consumers to take away and use: transferred from the computer of a faculty member to that of a student, along with a certificate of completion. This might sound cynical, but the advent of on-line degrees and courses facilitates this process. However, if you believe that management and managers have an impact on not just how people are treated in their immediate organization, but on the community and society at large, then critical thinking, moral debate, alternative and imaginative ways of thinking are key to managing organizations in responsible and responsive ways. Managers need to consider their role and responsibility in society; to consider not just the means of managing (the techniques), but the ends and the outcomes. And while research in sustainable management and corporate social responsibility has grown, as we will see in Chapter 5 it does not necessarily take a critical perspective.

In *Against Management* (2002), Martin Parker argues that CMS is basically a debate that takes place within the cloistered halls of academia and has had little impact on practice. But I suggest that it really depends upon how you teach CMS and whether you can engage management students in thinking differently about their experience. As managers and aspiring managers, students are often deeply enmeshed in prevailing managerial ideologies, structures of control and systems of power. And their career depends upon maintaining this system. CMS offers managers a basis for thinking differently about themselves and their organizational experience. It's this different way of thinking – about social and organizational life as emergent, socially constructed and inherently ideological and political – that encourages managers to challenge taken-for-granted organizational realities, places upon them a responsibility for relationships with others and forms the genesis for alternative 'realities'. As one of my Executive MBA (EMBA) students commented after completing a leadership course taught from a critical and a phenomenological perspective:

> Regarding your class ...
>
> I was a bit surprised that I actually enjoyed it. When I saw the syllabus, I was fairly certain I wouldn't get much out of it. Don't get me wrong, I still dislike writing long academic essays and cramming a ton of difficult reading into a few short weeks. But I probably never would have read [the course readings] on my own – I really enjoyed it and it helped me through some rough times these past few months ... I think you were the only professor in the programme who actually encouraged open dissent ... It was very refreshing.[12]

CMS does have something practical to offer managers – but it's a different practicality from the norm of technical rationality so prevalent in many business schools. It's a practicality based on the critical questioning of taken-for-granted practices and their impact, and it involves questioning not just the means of management, but also its ends.

However, CMS is not just suspicious about conventional management knowledge and practice, it should also be suspicious about itself. In other words, as CMS scholars we should walk the talk and question our own assumptions and practices if we believe knowledge is constructed, contested and speculative – because *all* forms of knowledge, whether conventional or critical, are constructed. This means being reflexive about our own practices.

## Summary

The purpose of this chapter has been to look at some of the ways that management and the role of managers have been constructed over the years. This history not only helps explain the current focus of management education and practice, but also illustrates its performative nature – that management, managerial roles and practices have are historically, culturally and linguistically influenced and have come into being through various management Discourses. We've also started to explore a more critical approach to management by looking first at the relationship between theory and practice and then at some of the main assumptions and concerns of Critical Management Studies.

Why is this background important? Because it illustrates how Discourses of management as rational, neutral and legitimate came into being and that traditional management curricula presuppose there is a right way of managing. The advent of Critical Management Studies drew attention to the need to question the impact of these Discourses and their underlying assumptions on managers, employees and society at large. As we will see in Chapter 3, more contemporary and critical ways of viewing managers as always *engaged in identity-work* offer not only a different way of thinking about what managers do and who they are, but also a different way of performing, *doing* and *becoming* a manager. But first we'll look at some basic assumptions about the nature of reality and language that underpin these alternative views. To return to the story of emergence and the landscape metaphor I used in the Introduction, we are going to look at the geology underlying the mountains, mesas and valleys.

## Notes

1.  See Chia and Morgan (1996); Ford and Harding (2007); French and Grey (1996); Ghoshal (2005); *Management Learning* Special Issue (2009); Parker (2002); and Willmott (1994).
2.  See Argyris (1982); Lawler (1985); Schön (1983); Vaill (1989); and Whetton and Cameron (1983).
3.  See Chapter 2 in Hatch with Cunliffe (2013) for a more detailed discussion of the history of Organization Studies, and Chapters 1 and 2 in Grey (2013) for further discussion on the Classical, Scientific Management and Human Relations schools.
4.  See Drucker (1973) for a discussion of the history, challenges and tasks of a manager.
5.  www.telegraph.co.uk/news/politics/9260245/Bloodless-bean-counters-rule-over-us-where-are-the-leaders.html (accessed 10 February 2013)
6.  See www.escpeurope.eu/escp-europe/history-of-escp-europe-business-school/ (accessed 4 September 2013).
7.  See Pfeffer and Fong (2002) for a brief history.
8.  For example, Hales (1986); Horne and Lupton (1965); Sayles (1964).
9.  See also: Alvesson and Willmott (1992, 1996); Grey and Willmott (2005); Harding (2003).
10. See www.youtube.com/watch?v=ts8JXuMN0Q4 (accessed 4 September 2013) for an example of Hopi leadership development.
11. Terms coined respectively by George Ritzer (1995) and Sharon Zukin (1996).
12. All quotes from students and managers are cited with permission.

# Communication, Language and Relational Managers

## Or 'That's Not What I Said ...'

I have held positions in community relations and economic development, relationships have always helped me to be successful on the
job. I had always viewed the other person from the outside, foster-
ing relationships in order to achieve a goal, make a sale, or build a
strategic partnership. I had never thought that I was just relying on
relationships as a means to an end. In fact, I never felt responsible
for these relationships, considered that others were all individuals
just like me, or took the time to understand their strengths and
values. (EMBA student)

This chapter examines some different ideas about the nature of reality and language. We will do so around the topic of communication,
which is seen as a key management competency. These ideas will
form the basis for understanding the Discourses of identity-work in
Chapter 3 and for developing the idea of managing as a relational
activity. We'll begin by looking at why conventional models of communication often fail and then examine some ideas about language
and the world that reveal a new landscape of possibilities for the way
we communicate with each other, not only in management, but in
every aspect of life. It's a way of thinking that grew out of a range of
disciplines, including philosophy, anthropology, sociology and, in particular, linguistics – disciplines that explore the different ways in which
we engage with our world. This might give you the impression that
what follows will be an extremely abstract and obtuse examination of
densely theoretical material. On the contrary, while it does involve
examining some basic philosophical, sociological and linguistic premises, our discussion is about everyday talk and the crucial nature of
language in the everyday life of any manager and employee. This is
based on the premise that every aspect of management involves language and communication, and that being aware of how language
works can enhance communication.

Why is communicating so problematic? How do we somehow manage to connect with each other and coordinate our actions in vaguely meaningful ways? The idea that our actions are only 'vaguely meaningful' might seem a particularly pessimistic view, but the difficulties of connecting were brought home a few years ago in a conversation with a US colleague who asked me (so I thought) how my daughter was. I said she was in the UK and not too happy. He asked if I'd 'had her flown out there' and what would I do if she 'had health problems'? He talked about how his 19-year-old died, and during the last year was so ill he didn't like to go on vacation and leave her with a sitter. Despite being perplexed by his turn of phrase, we continued talking for about 10 minutes – until we realized we were talking about two completely different things: he thought we were talking about dogs and I thought the conversation was about my daughter! Given the challenges of communicating, it's important for managers to understand and explore some very different ideas about what it is that we might be doing when we are communicating with organizational members.

## Questioning conventional models of communication and reality

No one would argue against the statement that communication is a crucial management skill, and any manager will tell you that she or he spends most of the day communicating with a wide variety of people, both within and outside the organization, on a range of issues including strategy, performance, financial reports, equipment breakdowns, and so on. Many will have studied communication as part of a management training and education programme. A quick Internet search on management communication reveals a vast number of courses on communication skills, listening techniques, body language, presentation skills, assertiveness, and the list goes on. Most management and organizational behaviour textbooks have at least one chapter on the topic, which usually defines communication as an exchange of information with the goal of achieving mutual understanding, and presents a model of the communication process that looks something like Figure 2.1.

So, given that there's a lot of stuff out there on communication, what more is there to say – forgive the pun – and what can be said that's any different? Is there anything that's not 'communication-as-usual' wrapped up differently?

I think there is. There's a different way of communicating that is not just another management technique, but involves a fundamentally different way of thinking about how language works and the nature of

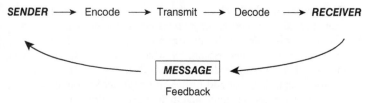

**Figure 2.1**  A model of the communication process

our relationships with other people. This different way of thinking about communication means we will encounter a strange world, a different 'language' and unfamiliar and curious forms of seeing, saying and doing. But I ask you to be open-minded about what follows, because I believe these ideas are crucial for the notion of managing as a relational activity and for the way managers interact with and manage people. Before we explore these ideas, let's unpack some taken-for-granted notions about communication – and this means that we need to address two main philosophical concerns and build on the ideas we discussed in Chapter 1: what is the nature of reality (*ontology*) and how do we understand and create knowledge about reality (*epistemology*)?

### Assumptions underlying conventional models

Figure 2.1 is not *just* a model of the communication process. Whether or not we realize it, the model also holds a number of assumptions about the nature of reality and language (*ontology*), how we make sense of reality and create knowledge (*epistemology*) and what ideal ways of communicating should look like. And because models and theories are performative, they constitute our way of communicating and relating to people. So what are these assumptions?

- First, that there is a *world out there* that exists separately from us, which we can all talk about and understand in the same way.
- That we can *represent* or accurately describe the world through language – as long as we use the correct language and get the communication process right.
- That a message contains words that mean some*thing*, they describe an object, an emotion, etc., and we all understand this meaning in the same way.
- That there are *independent* and *autonomous* senders and receivers, each with a message in mind that they want to convey to the other.

- The sender *first thinks* of what she or he wants to say and the best way of saying it (encodes) *before transmitting* the message.
- The receiver hears/reads the message and *decodes its real meaning.* If the receiver doesn't understand, for whatever reason, he or she will indicate this through feedback, which then enables the sender to rephrase the message or add further information. So communication is a recursive process culminating in an agreement over meaning.

These assumptions constitute what is known as a *realist* view of the world – that there is a real, independently existing reality and a particular way that humans live and communicate in the world. The consequences of realist assumptions for management is that communication is about the art of persuasion – of being able to use appropriate words and modes of transmission so that employees understand what you *really* mean, and being able to articulate a message in a persuasive way so they will actually do what you want them to do. As we will see later in this chapter and in Chapters 3 and 4, this understanding of reality and communication also carries implicit assumptions about rationality and power that are enacted in our day-to-day relations with others. But for the moment let's focus on what this model of communication takes for granted.

Is this how we actually communicate on a day-to-day basis? When we are talking to each other, do we deliberately and consciously formulate every sentence, or pause to decode what the other person is saying? Well yes, sometimes we might: if a manager is about to talk to an employee or a group of employees about budget deficits or changes to the marketing strategy, then she or he is likely to sit down and think about what they are going to say. But unless they actually write this down and read it word for word, then what they do say will be a mix of previously thought words and sentences, along with improvisations as they respond to the other person. And on a moment-to-moment basis we usually talk without any pauses in the conversation. In everyday conversations we respond to others in spontaneous and instinctive ways, and our conversations have an often unnoticed rhythm and flow, which gives us an overall sense and meaning. Let me give an example from a research conversation I had with a programme manager a few years ago. We were talking about some of the problems he dealt with on a day-to-day basis. Notice the rhythm of his words and how this supports what he's saying and reinforces an impression of the ambiguity of his job – an intuitive managing of meaning:

Problems are at a much higher level of abstraction; nothing is designed, nothing is given, everything is what you decide it is. If you ask somebody, 'What is this product going to do?' 'Well I don't know, you tell me.' 'When is it going to be finished?' 'Well I don't know – you tell me.' 'How much is it going to cost?' 'Well I don't know – you tell me ...'. (Originally cited in Cunliffe, 2002a)

This was part of a two-hour conversation, part of his normal way of talking and unrehearsed. Did he first think he would phrase his comment in this way and then say it? Listening to the audiotape, there was no pause before he spoke – he just continued to talk.

Interestingly, French philosopher Merleau-Ponty says, 'I do not speak *of* my thoughts; I *speak them,* and what is between them – my after-thoughts and underthoughts' (1964: 19). The point Merleau-Ponty is making is that we don't necessarily think *then* speak – we speak *and* think and often speak *then* think. So thinking and speaking are not separate activities but are somehow entwined and complete each other. To reinforce this point, next time you are having a conversation, try figuring out when you are speaking and when you are thinking – it's not easy! In this way, as Merleau-Ponty (1962) argues, language outruns us because we say more than we think and, as we talk and respond to each other, multiple meanings emerge. This can create problems if we assume that there's only one meaning (mine), it's the right meaning and that you just didn't understand what I was saying. This may explain why you often hear people say, 'But that's not what I said!', 'Why don't you listen?', or 'That's not what I asked you to do'!

So communication is not such a pre-planned, linear process as implied in Figure 2.1, and it's not just words that convey meaning. Before we explore communication and language further, I'd like to offer a different set of assumptions from the ones listed above. Assumptions which offer a basis for examining a different way of thinking about how we communicate, interact and relate with others. I'm going to spend a bit more time discussing these assumptions because they lay the foundation for the idea that managing is about how we relate to people and the world around us.

## Alternative ways of thinking about language, reality and communication ... and their impact on managing

The main point of this chapter is that language is a crucial yet often taken-for-granted aspect of managing organizations, crucial because everything a manager does involves some form of language – implementing strategy, monitoring budgets, encouraging people to work together, communicating goals, and so on. However, we need to move away from traditional ways of thinking about language and the belief that communication is an orderly, structured process in which we just have to select the correct words to describe accurately whatever it is that we are referring to. No, when we *live* language and communication, it's messier, fascinatingly complex, and our conversations are not wholly under our control. Yet, despite this, we somehow muddle through, we talk with other people and manage to get things done. But how?

Within the field of Organization Studies there lies a whole range of ideas about the nature and role of language in management: from the more conventional communication models as described in Figure 2.1, where language straightforwardly describes what is out there, to the idea that language is all there is, that is, that there is nothing – or no *thing* – outside language and that as humans we are just linguistic nodes, products of various discourses or ways of speaking. Let's look at some alternative ways of thinking about reality and language and why these might be of interest to managers. These ideas are linked to what's known as 'the linguistic turn', which focuses on the role of language in constituting organizational life. To do so we have to begin with the basic ontological question – what is the nature of social reality?

### So what is social 'reality'?

The world is wholly inside and I am wholly outside myself. (Merleau-Ponty, 1962: 474)

What if we move away from the realist view of the world and begin with the idea that social realities are not separate from people? What if we see ourselves and our world as intimately interwoven because each shapes and is shaped by the other in everyday interactions and conversations? In other words, we *talk* what we understand as our social world into existence and maintain 'its' existence in our talk, while at the same time what we believe is the outside social world plays back into what we do and say. To employ an academic label – realities are performatively and *socially constructed*. Let me illustrate this: two common terms used in organizations are human assets and human resources. How might employees be treated differently if they are labelled as human assets versus human resources?[1] And how might you be treated differently as an employee if you were seen as a human being? This is a good example of how words can shape actions. We might think and talk about the social world and organizations as being real and independent of whatever we say and do, but they take on a reality in our talk. The assumptions underlying this more critical construction of reality include:

- Our social world is *socially constructed*, created and maintained by us in our interactions and in turn influences the way we act and think, that is, the *human dialectic*.[2]
- We shape our social and organizational realities through language, e.g., *metaphors, speech genres*.
- Words have multiple meanings for different people and in different contexts – the arbitrary nature of *signifiers and signifieds*.
- In our living conversations no one person is in control of meaning because talk is *relationally-responsive* and meanings can be contested, i.e., *dialogism, heteroglossia*.
- We are not autonomous individuals but are always *in relation* to 'others' – to people, language, culture, the past/present/future …
- Thoughts and words are intertwined, so communication is not the linear 'think and then speak' process often depicted in textbooks.

M.C. Escher's lithograph *Drawing Hands* (1948) aptly captures the paradoxical nature of this view of social reality. You may recall that the lithograph is of two hands emerging from a sheet of paper, both holding pencils and drawing each other. Just as we ask how can two hands draw each other into existence – so we ask how can we shape a world that we think already exists? Merleau-Ponty discusses this at some length in *Phenomenology of Perception* (1962). He argues that there isn't an objective world out there that we each perceive in the same way, but that we and our world are *dialectically related*. What does this mean?

## We are our world and our world is us: social constructionism and dialectics

The idea of a socially constructed world gained attention with Berger and Luckmann's influential book, *The Social Construction of Reality* (1966), in which they proposed that society exists as both an objective and subjective reality. As they rather paradoxically stated: 'Society is a human product. Society is an objective reality. Man is a social product' (1966: 61) – which means that our social world is humanly produced in ongoing activity and routines, yet we experience it as being objective because it both affects our lives on an ongoing basis and we have to go out and learn about it. The importance of human interactions and relationships was highlighted by one of my EMBA students, who commented:

When a new staff person comes into an organization, where do their first perceptions come from? They don't come from something that they read. They come from what they hear and observe, how they are treated. In trying to understand how an organization's reality can be created from nothing, I could not help but think about a relationship between two people. Before you know each other there is no relationship. And then you get to know each other through interaction and it is almost like a third being comes alive. It is this living, breathing relationship in which there are elements of each person that are brought to the table and then new aspects of this relationship start to grow and mature. Ultimately, the people who know you accept this relationship and their perception of the relationship is what you have built by your actions.

She emphasizes the importance of relationships and conversations in shaping our world and interestingly talks about 'a third being', which we will discuss further on page 44. For French philosopher Merleau-Ponty, speech is originary and creative because it's how we talk things into being – just as a painter begins with a blank canvas and uses colour, form and space to create a work of art, so we create meaning and our experience of our world as we speak. And meaning is more than words, for just as a painting can evoke a range of emotions, so can our words – both may open up new ways of seeing, saying and acting: new possibilities for relating with others. We think, talk, argue, write, remember, love, manage and control others in language.

   This mutual relationship can be explained through the notion of *dialectics*. Dialectics is usually associated with dualisms – the idea that there are two opposing terms or situations that are perceived as irreconcilable, and so one is often chosen over the other. In management this may relate to quantity versus quality, centralization versus decentralization, a short-term versus a long-term orientation, rational versus emotional, and so on. Merleau-Ponty finds dualisms problematic: the idea that there is a separate mind and body, body and soul, reason and emotion, thought and speech, a person and a world ... This separation is known as Cartesian dualism, after the French philosopher René Descartes, who argued that mind and body are not the same and are in fact separate: the mind is intellectual, a consciousness without physical substance, whereas the body has substance – it takes up space but it doesn't think. Merleau-Ponty argued against these dualisms, suggesting that mind–body, person–world, you–I, and so on, are inseparable – are *dialectical*, which for Merleau-Ponty means two separate terms only becoming themselves through each other (Escher's *Drawing Hands*). So this forms a basis for the idea that managing is relational, it's not just about communicating, but is about how we see our relationship with the world and people around us.

For example, Merleau-Ponty suggests the *human dialectic* means that we create social (and organizational) structures and practices which exist in our interactions, but that we see as being independent from us and influencing, even determining, those actions. Consequently, these 'structures' can imprison us, they shape what we can and cannot do because we don't recognize that we ourselves create and maintain them in our actions and interactions. A good example of this is what Keenoy and Seijo (2009) call the 'double-edged character' of email because it makes communication easier and faster but is 'potentially addictive; endlessly demanding and opens us up to all sorts of uninvited communications' (2009: 188). We complain about never being free from it, yet carry our smart phone all the time and make sure our new email alert is on night and day. So it's a bit of a cop out when we – and organizational members – say we can't change things or deal with problems effectively because 'it's the system'. What is *the system*, who creates it and who keeps it going? Are we imprisoned by the view that the system is real and exists independently from us? This is why it's important to see and understand this continually changing dialectical relationship and the part we play.

You might be raising your eyebrows rather cynically at this point ... Where is this going and how does it relate to managers? The person–world dualism has implications for how we view and manage organizations. For example, the idea that managers should be rational is typical of Cartesian dualism: emotions (the body) should not interfere with the rational working of the mind, because emotion is irrational and impacts our ability to be objective. As we will see in the following chapters, there's more than one rationality and what is objective to me might seem completely arbitrary to you.

Let's begin to look at the human dialectic in management and organizational terms. Organizations don't exist by themselves, but in the interactions and conversations and activities of organizational members. That's not to say that there aren't physical aspects of organizations – of course there are buildings, machines, desks and products. But what gives the organization its identity and managers their authority? How do people do their work and coordinate their actions, and how do products and services come into being? Formal policies, operating procedures and job descriptions do have some sort of 'thingness' or materiality because they are words on paper – but they exist and take on meaning as people talk and act in relation to them. Job descriptions, for example, are maintained through our everyday activities, through common ways of talking and through routine behaviours and interactions. Job descriptions don't *do* things by themselves. This requires a shift in thinking, because it means seeing the world existing in social interactions and relationships rather than in structures and systems. And while cultural anthropologists and sociologists such as Clifford Geertz (1983), James Clifford (1983) and George Marcus (1986) have long questioned our relationship with our social world and the ways in which we account for our experience, the majority of research in Management and Organization Studies still takes a realist perspective by studying organization structures, systems and management roles, and by identifying the laws, principles and norms that influence human behaviour. But do such laws and principles *really* exist or are they constructed by academics to explain our world?

Berger and Luckmann's main premise, that social realities and identities are created and maintained in conversations and social interactions rather than in structures, has been taken up by scholars in a number of disciplines, who have developed the notion that social reality, identities and knowledge are culturally, socially, historically and linguistically influenced. In Chapter 3, we will see how this idea helps construct management in different ways through the idea of managers as storytellers, managers of meaning and reflexive authors. And we'll explore what this means for managing organizations and for organizational culture in Chapter 4. But for now let's focus on language and the relational nature of reality.

## How does language work?

This brings us to our next main premise – that language doesn't represent the world, it *is* our world because we cannot separate language, ourselves and the world: they exist in a mutual relationship. As Michael Agar says in *Language Shock*, 'They're wrapped up together like hydrogen and oxygen in water. You can't pull them apart and still have the water to drink' (1994: 66). Okay, let's say you buy in, at least a little bit, to this idea – that we shape our social realities through language – then what is language, how does it work and why do managers need to think about language? If language doesn't describe things, then what does it do and how does it shape our world? This is where we are going to get into some pretty complex ideas about the nature of language, but I want to ground these as much as possible in practical examples from managers, because this is the point – language *is* our experience.

I'd like to go back to the research I did for my PhD, because this was when the importance of language first struck me. One of my research sites was a small US manufacturing organization. I had an initial conversation with the president of the company before talking to the senior managers, spending time in the organization and talking to first line supervisors on workshops. In our initial taped conversation, the president commented:

> I live in this world of uncertainty. I am not naive any longer – I come in in the morning now and I'm a skeptic. I say, 'Okay, first tell me about all the casualties, I want to set priorities. What are the things that might take us out of business today?' I'm not being wise, I'm being a realist ... Right now we're wrestling with keeping two boilers up and running ...

I didn't really think about the language he used until listening to tapes of my conversations with other members of the organization. It was then I began to realize that there seemed to be a common way of speaking about the organization that gave me a sense of the organization as a battlefield. Indeed the president had used this term on a number of occasions. The battlefield *metaphor* played through my conversations with other managers and employees, who used words like 'shotgun approaches', 'keep them in our camp', 'stay on your toes' and 'run up the red flag'. Such metaphors can be very powerful in shaping the ways in which people talk, think and act, because a shared common sense emerges about the nature of organizational life. If a senior manager comes in every day and asks about 'casualties', he or she will be told what all the problems are. Pretty soon this will be part of everyday ways of talking in the organization. And employees will see this as being what the organization is *really* like – which will continue to influence their ways of talking and acting ... Precisely the *Drawing Hands* paradox and Merleau-Ponty's human dialectic!

What's interesting is that this is usually not obvious to organizational members. I had a final meeting with the president when I showed him a transcript of our conversations and asked him about his comments. He was shocked, he hadn't realized he was using this language, nor had he thought about its impact. He asked what he could do? What about if he came in every morning and asked what was going well and what could be built upon and improved? How might that influence the way people talked about and perceived the organization?

I've cited the conversation with the president and other managers before, because they are wonderful examples of the powerful, sedulous and sometimes insidious nature of language (Cunliffe, 2001, 2002a, 2002b). Yes, managers think about how to phrase mission and vision statements, or what words to use in formal statements and written documents – but they don't always think about what they say in conversations or about the powerful nature of everyday ways of speaking. The example above illustrates a point made by Merleau-Ponty that, 'Speech is, therefore, that paradoxical operation through which, by using words of a given sense, and already available meanings, we try to follow up an intention which necessarily outstrips, modifies, and in itself, in the last analysis, stabilizes the meanings of the words which translate it' (1962: 452). In other words, the president was using familiar words, but by his use of these particular words in this context, and the way others understood and responded to his use of these words, stable meanings and ways of acting emerged that he did not necessarily intend. And all this was not a conscious process, nor was it under any one person's control, it happened over time and in many conversations. Did he intend to convey a sense of the organization as a chaotic battlefield? No, but this is what emerged – his words outstripped him! And this goes on every day in all organizations, in conversations about strategy, about the provision of services, market brand, improving team performance … You can begin to understand the crucial influence of everyday ways of talking by looking at how organizational members talk: the words, phrases, metaphors they use and how these relate to the way things are done. Language works in subtle ways, which is why managers need to move beyond the conventional model of communication based on an objective reality (Figure 2.1) to understand the power of their words in constructing social realities.

You might be getting the idea that the world is *only* about language, or that anything goes – that we can say and therefore create absolutely anything. There are some scholars, mainly poststructuralists, who think language is all there is. But for the moment let's begin with some less radical ideas about the nature of language and how it works.

Linguists study language. The father of modern linguistics is Ferdinand de Saussure, a Swiss linguist whose teachings were compiled by his students in the 1959 book *Course in General Linguistics* (first published in 1911). Saussure wished to study language scientifically, to describe how language existed at particular points in time. But he realized that he could not study speech itself (*la parole*), because the spoken word is too idiosyncratic, too full of hesitations and reformulations. Yet, at any one moment in time, people have knowledge of grammatical forms of talk as a result of their shared use of language (*la langue*). So he felt our *knowledge of language* is very orderly and could be studied in a systematic manner. When we are presented with various sentences and asked to judge whether or not they are grammatically correct, we can do so. We know which words are 'proper' and which are not, and we know how words have to be used in particular ways in a sentence. Remember English grammar at school and the exercise of mapping sentence structures? This is known as *prescriptive* linguistics because it's concerned with how we *should* speak – and while prescriptive linguistics might define what is acceptable, our everyday use of language is not that precise! You might remember one of the famous catchphrases of British comedians Eric Morecambe and Ernie Wise, 'The play what I wrote'. There's no way this can be seen as the correct way of talking, but it was a way of talking that Morecambe and Wise drew upon precisely because it's very unacceptability made a humorous point in that particular dramatic context – that ostensibly Ernie thought his rather ambitious, badly written and trite plays were really good – and the phrase made its way into everyday conversation and popular culture at that time. Another such example is UK comedienne Catherine Tate's 'Am I bovvered?'.

So not only is language fascinatingly complex, it's also very clever, and we understand this intuitively and engage in its multifariousness on a day-to-day basis. A number of organizational scholars have studied this aspect of language in an organizational context. Mary Jo Hatch (1997) studied how a team of managers engaged in irony as a means of understanding and dealing with the complexities of organizational life. She suggested that irony offers a way of grappling with possibilities and impossibilities because of its contradictory nature, and because it engages humour and emotion that can lend a sense of sharing – of being in this together – that might otherwise be difficult to create. This shared meaning is not explicitly agreed, it just happens, and it has an impact on the way we feel about the organization or situation. One organization I worked for years ago was experiencing a leadership crisis and a colleague made the comment, 'All we need now is for X to step up to the plate!' Of course, this was the last thing we wanted because X would cause even more havoc and conflict, but the ensuing laughter relieved tension and, as Hatch suggests, allowed new constructions of the future to take place in a less threatening atmosphere. Bakhtin argues that irony is a way of rising above a situation and that, 'Only dogmatic and authoritarian cultures are one-sidedly serious' (1986: 134). So managers need to be aware that it's not just formal and prescriptive language that shapes meaning – but that informal everyday ways of talking can have much more of an impact than they might imagine. And their everyday talk impacts relationships and how organizational members relate to each other.

## Words have different meanings

Saussure also described language as a system of *signs*, letters and words that we string together in particular ways to make sentences that mean something. Signs consist of *signifiers* (the shape and sound of a word, e.g., t-a-b-l-e) and *signifieds* (the object or concept that the signifier is about), and it's when the signifiers and signified come together that the sign takes on some kind of meaning. If you hear someone say the word 'table' (the signifier), you have an idea of what that actually means – a square wooden object with four legs (the signified). But as we have seen, language isn't that simple! When hearing 'table', you might think of a round glass table with a central marble stand, a stainless steel writing table, a small rectangular coffee table ... and so the relationship between signifiers and signified can be *arbitrary* because signifiers have a number of different meanings. I can of course be more specific and say, 'Last night I went to dinner with three friends and we sat around a wonderful small oval antique wooden table with ....', but this is still open to interpretation (how small, what type of wood, and so on). However, the example does bring us to another point Saussure made – that it's the *relationship between signs in a sentence* that helps create meaning, not the words themselves. We use the same words in many different contexts in which the meaning varies – 'I'll *tell* you what to do', 'I couldn't *tell* them apart', 'I'm going to *tell* on you', 'It was a *tell-all* book'. In these examples, *tell* variously means inform, distinguish, report, reveal. It's the context in which the words are used, the sentence and the situation that give words and signs meaning. Saussure believed this is why we needed to develop a language system to explain how signs are organized into meaning and how language works.

Not only are there many possible meanings of signifiers, but situations become more arbitrary at times when signifiers and signified don't connect. This was made patently clear to me during a five-hour bus trip through Mexico to visit a friend. I spoke no Spanish and no one on the bus spoke English. I could hear the signifiers (the words) but had no clue what they meant. I coped with the few stops in the journey by watching everyone else, tagging along at the back and making sure I didn't wander too far from the bus because I'd no idea what time it would leave. My inability to combine signifiers and signified into meaningful signs became more problematic at the end of the trip. I'd expected to arrive at a bus station where I would meet my friend, but the driver dropped people off at their houses and obviously wanted to do the same for me. We gave up trying to communicate and thankfully he drove to the bus garage where I found somebody who spoke a little English and phoned my friend. This example illustrates another key aspect of Saussure's work – that meaning emerges in language use or in actual speech (*parole*): signs and social life are intimately connected and language use is culture and community specific. This has implications for managing because it implies that written words (e.g., vision and mission statements) are not enough, we talk through and create shared meanings about goals, strategy and values, etc., in our everyday conversations. We can also identify particular forms of discourse in organizations, which often don't make sense to new employees or to people outside the organization such as customers, patients, suppliers, etc.

And we are not just talking about different languages, but the use of language in different cultures and contexts. When I first moved from the UK to the US, I discovered the normal response to 'Hi, how are you?' was not the typically British 'Oh, not too bad', because this caused the inquirer to stop in their tracks. A perky 'Fine, how are you?!' was expected. It actually took me a number of years to manage this reply because the other was so deeply ingrained and habitual. I was equally astounded that US managers often used the phrase 'No problem' in response to requests to do something, without seeming to assess first whether or not it would be a problem. I was more familiar with UK manager responses, which were usually more tentative in nature. Of course misunderstandings arise when we have to work in different cultures without realizing that different linguistic conventions and embedded ways of talking exist, and that they are performative because we begin to make judgements that affect how we interact with people. For example, the perception that US managers are brash and want to do things now, so don't consult them until you've considered all your options, versus UK managers who never give you a straight answer and play for time, so it's better just to get the job done yourself. Okay, while these might be (not entirely unfamiliar) extremes, my point is that it's important for managers to be reflexively aware of different ways of talking and the impact on everyday interaction. This requires paying attention not only to what we say, but also to what we assume, and one of the main assumptions we need to question is that we all understand things in the same way.

## Language, living conversations and relationality

In the first edition of this book, I introduced the notion of relational managers. Since then, I have been developing further the idea of relationality – the idea that we are always in relation to others (people, language, culture, etc.) whether or not we realize it. A few years ago, a colleague and I interviewed Federal Security Directors (FSDs) – a position created to establish security at US airports after September 11. Many of the FSDs talked about the importance of establishing relationships, being responsive to people (e.g., employees, passengers, the FBI, airport employees) and being respectful to others (Cunliffe and Eriksen, 2011). One FSD commented:

> When you get to an airport, you tend to be nervous, you're not sure what to do, you're not sure where to go. So we've picked out people that have shown this ability to communicate effectively and connect with people. They'll start talking to people, 'How are you ma'am? Where are you heading today? You know, you're in a long line, why don't you just sit down there ... Just check your bag right here and you're going to be okay ...'. You see the stress level go right down! The Airport Director goes to Washington often ... he loves to talk about relationships, partnerships, and dealing with the way we've been able to solve problems.

As the FSD says, communication is not just about talking to people, but connecting with them and establishing relationships. It's the latter that's often forgotten or ignored in conventional models of communication, which focus mainly on how managers can communicate their ideas more effectively and 'use direct persuasion' (Hay Group, 2001) so that they can link the performance of employees to organizational goals. Of course establishing relationships and being respectful of people sounds like common sense, but I want to suggest that the persuasive communication techniques that form the basis of many management training programmes can lead to individualistic and egocentric attitudes which result in managers blaming others because they've misunderstood. They can even result in the manipulation and bullying of employees.

I've tried to emphasize the role that language plays in everything we do and want to go on to explore in more depth why this is crucial to managing people and organizations. This is also where we'll begin to connect to the idea of managing as relational practice: that whatever managers do, it is not in isolation, but always in relation to other people, to communities and to ways of talking.

Saussure's ideas were taken up, developed and challenged by other linguists across a range of disciplines including psychology, sociology and Organization Studies. While his work was incredibly influential in drawing attention to language use and the idea that speech is creative, unique and individual, he was more concerned with identifying general language systems. It was this interest that led to the development of *semiotics*, an emerging field in Organization Studies with particular relevance for understanding organizational culture. We will explore semiotics further in Chapter 4. But it was Mikhail Mikhalovich Bakhtin, a Russian literary theorist, who took up what Saussure had thought too complex to study: speech and the act of speaking itself. Bakhtin found the notion of linguistic systems and linguistic analysis problematic, because they focused on 'the relationships among elements within the language system' (1986: 118) and ignored real conversations, real people and the responsive nature of understanding and meaning. I'd like to pick up three aspects of his work because they have particular relevance for the ways in which we manage people and organizations: dialogism, speech genres and heteroglossia.

## Living conversations: dialogism and speech genres

> Dialogue here is not the threshold to action, it is the action itself. It is not a means for revealing, for bringing to the surface the already ready-made character of a person; no, in dialogue a person not only shows himself outwardly, but he becomes for the first time that which he is – and, we repeat, not only for others but for himself as well. To be means to communicate dialogically. When dialogue ends, everything ends. (Bakhtin, 1984: 262)

Bakhtin's idea that dialogue is the way in which we become who we are is, for me, central to identity-work and relational managing. This is contrary to the model of communication in Figure 2.1, which is about revealing 'ready-made' realities, identities and meanings. As you might imagine from the quote above, Bakhtin was interested in exploring ways of thinking about *living speech*, that is, how we actually speak to each other (Saussure's *la parole*), in all its living detail. You rarely come across his work in management literature and on management courses, which is a pity because he offers a number of insights into how we live our lives with others. One theme running through his work that particularly fascinates me is his idea that we are always in relation to an 'other': a particular person, a context, a way of speaking and a culture. This means that we do not have complete freedom or control in what we say and, I suggest, means that *we therefore have a responsibility to consider 'others' as we speak.*

Let's begin with *dialogism*. Bakhtin (1986) differentiated between monologic and dialogic language. Think of a monologue in a play – a speech by one actor to other actors or to the audience – which captures a number of elements of Bakhtin's monologism: a single *author*ity who is unresponsive to how his or her voice is being received, a particular view or ideology, and an aim of coming to a common understanding of a pre-established view. We typically think of this way of relating as autocratic management. Bakhtin criticized the oppressive nature of monologic discourse, suggesting that it rules out diverse meanings and silences other voices. He argued that we need to focus on the *dialogic* aspect of language as living utterances – the two-way movement of dialogue between people in particular moments and particular settings. Dialogism takes into account 'others' because it means recognizing that meaning emerges in the 'interaction and struggle' (1986: 92) of back-and-forth conversation between people. This struggle occurs in the specific moments of conversation, but these moments also occur within a general context of wider meanings. He explained this relationship by suggesting that our conversations consist of a person who speaks, a person who listens (the addressee), and a *superaddressee*, an invisible third agency that exists outside the conversation. The superaddressee is not necessarily another person, but is rather a need to be understood by others beyond the immediate conversation; by a person, a group of people, a community, and so on – to whom or to which we must be *responsive* and *responsible* in our talk. For example, when a group of senior managers are engaged in discussion about, let's say, business strategy or market brand, they need to consider not only the other listeners in the room, but be responsive to the needs and understandings of the superaddressee (shareholders, customers, the local community, the media, etc.). So what we say both has meanings unique to the context in which we speak and carries with it broader meanings that need to be understood by others who may not be present at the time of speaking. Dialogism means being open to others, to various voices and meanings, and to the need for dialogue and discussion as integral to responsive and ethical management. *Thus, dialogue and dialogism are central concerns of relational managers and leaders* (Cunliffe and Eriksen, 2011).

Monologic and dialogic ways of talking have implications for managing organizations and for organizational culture because much of the official and formal communication that goes on in organizations is of a monologic form. Mission, vision and value statements are designed to create a single unified meaning and to direct the behaviour of employees. Courses on management communication often incorporate techniques such as framing and impression management – ways not only of presenting information but also of presenting ourselves to others in order to influence their perceptions of us in a favourable way. According to Fairhurst and Sarr (1996) framing is an essential leadership skill involving the use of language to shape the way in which people interpret and give meaning to situations, and this is crucial because meaning influences action. Impression management is also about shaping meaning in a wider sense; not just through language but also by constructing a desirable social identity by presenting ourselves and our organizations in a positive way

(Highhouse, Brooks and Gregarus, 2009; Kakabadse, Bank and Vinni-combe, 2004). These are monologic forms of communication because they aim to impose a particular meaning on others. However, they often fail in this aim because different people have different *interpretations* of what is being said, what is written and how we act. We will explore the implications of monologism for managing organizations further in Chapter 4. Meanwhile, consider the potentially misleading, insincere and manipulative nature of such forms of monologic discourse and how people respond to this. And consider how much of the conversation that goes on in organizations is monologic or is genuinely dialogic.

Bakhtin (1986) also suggested that all human activity involves language and that language consists of relatively stable ways of speaking used in particular contexts. These stable ways of speaking become obvious when you move into new or different contexts. As a manager you will find yourself using 'management' language (bottom line, deliverables, metrics) and as a student of management, you probably find yourself having to talk about mimetic isomorphism, LMX theory and poststructuralism, etc., in class. My point is that there are different ways of speaking that occur in different contexts: business, technical, scientific, academic, legal, etc. Bakhtin calls these different ways of speaking *speech genres*, which consist of:

a) primary speech genres – the simple, unmediated utterances of everyday conversation, and

b) secondary speech genres – the complex, organized, ideological, premeditated forms of communication we find in scientific research, novels and formal organization documents and statements. Academic journal articles and business presentations are just two examples of secondary speech genres that use specific forms of language.

While secondary speech genres can be useful in shortcutting long explanations within professional groups, Bakhtin argues that they lose our immediate relation to reality because they reduce complex and ever-changing experience to a particular logic, category or theoretical forms of talk. A profit and loss account, a company annual report and an organization's strategy document are all examples of secondary speech genres that can and do simplify and mask the challenges and complexities of everyday organizational life. Have you ever sat in class listening to someone talk about planning techniques, strategic analysis or six principles for building and motivating teams, and thought – if only life was that simple?!

So what does this mean for managers and managing organizations? In *In Search of Management* (2001), Tony Watson talks about two competing languages in the organization he studied. One, an official language represented in formal documents, was about empowerment and growth (monologic, secondary speech genres), the other was the unofficial language of how managers actually spoke to each other on a day-to-day basis (dialogic, primary speech genres), and was about the pressure they felt in trying to control costs and jobs. He found that while some managers operated in either the official or the unofficial language, others switched confusingly between the two. Part of the official language involved talking about 'skill grades' instead of 'jobs', but Watson found there was resistance to this monologic 'language reform' by managers who continued to use the 'illegal language' (2001: 115).

Dialogic and monologic ways of talking, primary and secondary speech genres therefore play through and influence our ways of talking, often without us realizing it. Which takes us back to Merleau-Ponty's idea that language does things in specific moments but also works beyond us. These ideas also highlight the importance of thinking about how we relate to others: the day-to-day impact of what we say (and write), about what meanings we impose, who we exclude or allow to speak and how people respond. Which brings us to the next assumption underlying this way of thinking about communication – that our conversations are not about a linear encoding and decoding of information, but about creating meaning as we relate and respond to each other.

### Relationally-responsive conversations

The notion of speech genres also highlights the notion that making sense of what's going on around us is not just an intellectual activity taking place inside our heads using theory and models, but it is a practical, relational, responsive activity occurring in our everyday conversations. So reading a book about management techniques, or having a policy document or mission statement (both secondary speech genres) only goes so far – it's what we do and say (primary speech genres) that counts. It's in our living dialogic relationships, our relationally-responsive interaction, that we create meanings, make sense of what's happening around us and work out what needs to be done (Cunliffe, 2008; Shotter and Cunliffe, 2002).

Let me give an example from my own research. We typically think of research interviews (structured or unstructured) as involving carefully worded questions, that is, as a monologic and secondary speech genre. But the answers to our questions are unscripted and we often find ourselves working out meaning with our research 'subjects' depending on the dialogic overtones and nuances of our utterances, that is, as a primary speech genre. Notice in the excerpt below from one of my research conversations how Paul and I respond to each other:

Paul: I was just recently approached by the EDA, saying would I mind joining the board of directors? ... These are the sorts of things ... ummm ... I have to start positioning myself and it creates a little anxiety because it's like, you know, I'll be leaving the store – is it okay? Is the support there? Is the organization up to the level it should be?

Ann: So the anxiety is about what you're leaving, not what you're going to?

Paul: Yes. I'll be honest with you, a morning like today, I've enjoyed because it's stimulating, and I've done this with the managers, when you pull them away. We go to [offsite] – you've been there – or somewhere, and you talk about the business objectives. It allows you to kind of assess, look forward, and when you're there it's almost like unreal ... you know [at work] you're in a meeting and phones are ringing and there's someone in the office and you ... Well, you'll see – we can't be accused of high overheads! [Laughs] We're on one another's shoulders, worrying about what's in ...

Ann: So on site it's easy to be managed by the detail?

Paul: Yes ... we've no closed doors. But when I really have something I want to sit down and focus on ... right now we need to understand our competitors, one of whom has been taken over by the Japanese, which may mean we have to become more aggressive.

Ann: Will this have a big impact on the business?

Paul: There'll be further decline – even if it's 5 per cent but it's only going to go so far, there'll always be a need for the product. I don't know if we want to position ourselves as the buggy whip in manufacturing but we'll survive, and we'll have the best organization in place, and no one else is around at our price.

This excerpt illustrates the relationally-responsive nature of dialogue and the importance of speech genres in making sense. To use Bakhtin's terms, Paul and I are actively responding to each other's comments, and not only does Paul explain in response to my questions, but he tries to orient me ('a morning like today', 'you've been there'), builds on utterances ('you know, you're in a meeting ...'), and anticipates ('Well, you'll see ...). In this way, I'm an *active other* throughout the conversation, even though I may not be speaking at that moment. Paul draws on both primary ('phones are ringing') and secondary ('business objectives', 'overheads') speech genres. I later drew on secondary academic speech genres relating to my research interests and a super-addressee (academics) – as I am right now – to anticipate how I might write up the research. This excerpt also illustrates what Bakhtin calls the *expressive* aspect of dialogue – our emotional and evaluative connections to what (and to whom) we are talking.

What this suggests is that contrary to the archetype of the rational manager who stands back and assesses situations objectively, whether we are conscious of it or not, every statement – its content and the way it's said – is expressive. As Bakhtin says, 'There can be no such thing as an absolutely neutral utterance' (1986: 84). Would Paul have exactly the same conversation, use the same words and say them in the same way to a different person? I doubt it. So the rational and the relationally-responsive manager are two very different beings, and the relational view of managing goes beyond managers as storytellers and managers of meaning because while the latter implies some individual control over meaning, managing in a relational way accepts that meanings are shaped *between* people in conversations and shift with conversations. Relational managers therefore focus on dialogue (talking with) rather than monologue (talking to).

So how does relationally-responsive dialogue differ from the realist communication model we began with in Figure 2.1? This approach to language and communication is based on a different set of ontological assumptions: conversations are not about what exists and about finding the right words to convey the correct meaning – but about shaping meanings, understandings and social realities *between us as we talk and respond to each other*. It's not about imposing meaning on others (monologue) but about dialogue, responsiveness and movement. Meaning does not lie in the words themselves, but in how we use words and put them together in a particular conversation – a conversation in which no one person has control because each is responding to the other with a superaddressee in mind. And such meaning is never final-ized as something objective, but shifts within and across conversations.

Rather than focus on an external model of communication, it is important for managers to think about how they actually talk and relate to people on a moment-to-moment basis. How might what I say, how I say it and how I interact with someone influence his or her response and the meanings and understandings emerging between us? This is not a prescriptive approach to communication, it does not involve defining and using a language system, but it is *a reflexive and responsive approach*. It means being more careful and thoughtful about our everyday conversations because we recognize that we are (dialectically) shaping ever-changing and unfinished meanings and 'realities' in our dialogue.

### Conversations are about differences and similarities: heteroglossia

Which brings us to the third point I wish to draw from Bakhtin's work (1981): that language is *heteroglossic*. Heteroglossia, literally *multi-speechedness*, suggests that language is a complex mix of different types of speech: everyday speech and language systems, primary and secondary speech genres, national and local ways of talking, different styles, intonations, expressions, social and historically based ways of talking, and different worldviews or ideologies. Rather like having a group of rock, hip hop, rap, electronic, punk and classical musicians in a room together! These differences work both to resist or pull apart (centrifugal forces) meaning and to unify (centripetal forces) them. Remember Tony Watson's example of the two languages? Both the official and unofficial language exemplified centripetal and centrifugal forces: the unofficial language of managers both resisted and unified meanings by challenging and destabilizing the official organization language and creating a very different common unofficial language.

Rational managers communicate and act mainly based on centripetal forces, because they want to regulate and control behaviour and employees to speak the language of the organization. Managers who are storytellers and managers of meaning, as we will see in the next chapter, also often use language in a centripetal sense – to unify meaning and values and action. For example, in an attempt to motivate staff a manager may tell a heroic story about everyone pulling together to get the work done, however, staff treat the story with disdain because they interpret it as a weak attempt to control and manipulate them. These are centrifugal forces leading to different versions of the story, different meanings and sometimes resistance.

Relational managers need to be attuned to heteroglossia, to recognize and work with the differences and similarities of many voices. To illustrate how this might occur within everyday conversations, I'd like to take as an example an imaginary project planning meeting between a department manager (DM) and her or his member of staff (MS). The dialogue might go along the lines of:

DM: Look, the bottom line is that these are the deliverables that have to be met. We have to create a product spec and product development process by June because they need to be incorporated in the operations manual. Production needs the specs to re-tool and start scheduling material deliveries. We agreed this a month ago.

MS: Yes, but Engineering haven't come up with the technical specs yet, and until they do we can't work on the product specs. I talked to one of the engineers, Dave, who told me he can't do anything as Phil [the engineering manager] told him to hold off ... I talked to Phil and *he* just came up with a list of reasons why they can't get the specs to us by the end of the month.

DM: It's his job! They held up the last project because they refused to accept our authority. He has to accept that's the authority structure.

MS: I think part of Phil's reluctance is that we've not been communicating the complexity of the project, so he doesn't understand the cost when they kick up a fuss for a week. I talked to R&D yesterday to get their input, and they are perfectly willing to help, but they want to be involved in planning discussions like these. If other departments were involved and part of the planning process they would feel taken care of and there'd be more buy-in ...

DM: It's not my job to mollycoddle people. I'll get on to Engineering and tell them we need the information by the end of the week ... I'm ultimately responsible for this project. Engineering just want their little fiefdom and need to realize my tolerance for stalling is low. They need to get moving.

There's a failure to understand the heteroglossic nature of dialogue on the part of DM, who assumes that everyone should see the situation the same way, and wants his or her voice to predominate. MS is far more attuned to heteroglossia: the different voices, meanings ('taken care of' versus 'mollycoddling'), ideas and speech types, and to the need to work towards the active understanding of the other (the engineering manager). Crucially, for Bakhtin, communication means dialogue – speaking *with* others in which all participate as equals – rather than rhetoric – speaking *to* others to persuade them. See if you can notice heteroglossia and the difference between the dialogism and monologism (or rhetoric) in your own conversations, or by observing conversations of others.

### And so to relationality...

Let's summarize these complex ideas and their implications for communication. Communication as living conversations means understanding that:

- Meanings and organizational 'realities' emerge between people in everyday interactions and relationally-responsive conversations – and shape our understandings and actions.
- We need to pay attention to the nature of everyday conversations – to emerging similarities and differences as people interpret words, actions and conversations in various ways, have different ways of talking and draw on various speech genres.
- Monologism supports one way of thinking and suppresses different voices, views and creativity. Dialogism acknowledges, supports and works with cultural, ideological and personal differences and emphasizes the importance of relationships.

Medvedev and Bakhtin talk about *speech tact* playing through every conversation, which is a rather nice way of thinking about these issues. Tact is not just politeness but being attuned to 'the social relationships of the speakers, their ideological horizons, and, finally, the concrete situation of the conversation' (1978: 95). But what does this actually mean in practice and why is this way of thinking about language and communication important? It means that we need to view communication as shaping meaning *together* as we speak. It means paying much more attention to 'others' in our everyday conversations: what we say, the words we use, how we speak, how people may respond to us and how we respond to them. It means questioning how monologic forms of talk and secondary speech genres may exclude others and limit our choices. And it means that managers need to think about what they do as always in relation to other people, and to carefully consider what they want that relationship to be. This is the basis for managing relationally.

### Summary

I started this chapter by suggesting that language and communication are incredibly important to managers, but that traditional models can be problematic because they are based on specific assumptions that offer a particular view of the world that may be a limited and possibly manipulative one. We then looked at some different ideas about the nature of language and its relationship to social reality, which require us to reassess the way we communicate. From a social constructionist perspective, language dialectically shapes and is shaped by our social and organizational realities. Language is also complex because meanings are arbitrary – depending on the moment and context in which we speak, listen, write and read. While meanings differ in each moment of speaking, there are particular ways of talking (secondary speech genres) that influence what we say. Our everyday conversations are relationally-responsive and therefore never under the control of one person.

We therefore need to be aware of the subtle and powerful ways in which language influences our lives: of its limiting and enlightening consequences. We will explore some of these consequences in the following chapters. For the moment I suggest that language isn't all there is – we live, feel, act, laugh, but we cannot escape its grasp because our actions and emotions take on meaning in language and help us connect with others. When we hear someone say 'I am angry' or 'I love you', we have a sense of what the person is feeling, even though 'anger' and 'love' might be expressed and felt differently. So let's be optimistic – language doesn't imprison us and determine everything we do or say. Rather it's a 'familiar room', carrying 'with it patterns of seeing, knowing, talking, and acting' (Agar, 1994: 71) that both shape what we say, do and who we are, and also offer possibilities for change.

### Notes

1. I'm indebted to an unknown person who made this comment at a conference a number of years ago.
2. See Matt Koschmann's Vimeo, *What Is Organizational Communication?* Available at: http://vimeo.com/40984192 (accessed 6 September 2013).

# Who are Managers?
# Discourses of Identity-Work

In this chapter we will begin to take a more critical perspective by looking at different Discourses – ways of thinking about and constructing – managers and their identity-work, each based on alternative assumptions about the nature of social and organizational realities. These various ways of theorizing highlight the complexities of being a manager and offer ways of rethinking who managers are and who they could be.

Chapter 1 offered probably the most common definition of managers – as members of the organization who get things done through other people. This sounds incredibly simple, but if you speak to anyone who is a manager they will tell you that the devil is in the detail … in other words it's easier said than done! We also looked at some of the early studies of the roles and work activities of managers (Table 1.1), many of which still form the basis for management training and development activities today. This work draws mainly on a functionalist perspective, which assumes there is a real social reality 'out there' with roles and accepted ways of behaving into which we have to be socialized in order to be good members of organizations and society.

While much of management theory and education in the latter half of the twentieth century (and still today) is about constructing the 'ideal' goal-oriented manager, CMS highlights the problematic nature of this task. Critical studies of managers and management are often based on two assumptions: managing is about identity-work and is performative.

## Managing as identity-work

This is the notion that being a manager and developing a management career is not about performing pre-determined and regulated roles, but is about identity-work – how managers actively try to shape their identities and make their presence meaningful to themselves and others. So what is the difference between the role-based studies we saw in Chapter 1 and the identity-work studies we will now examine? Roles are often generalized across individuals as relatively fixed categories (e.g., Mintzberg's disturbance handler and negotiator) within which managers have to act. They often become ideals that are used to judge whether someone is a good member of society or an effective manager. Identity-work is a more 'wholistic' and fluid concept, concerned with a whole person, based on each individual's life history and, as we will see, is *always emerging* within our interactions. It therefore makes sense to talk about managers in terms of their identity-work rather than fixed managerial roles.

Tony Watson defines identity-work as 'the mutually constitutive process in which people strive to shape a relatively coherent and distinctive notion of personal self-identity and struggle to come to terms with and, within limits, to influence the various social identities which pertain to them in the various milieux in which they live their lives' (2008: 129). In other words, we try to shape a coherent sense of our identity as we try to balance the expectations relating to the 'social identities' (e.g., manager, student, mother, accountant) that relate to us, with our everyday experience and our own sense of self – not always easy to do! Notice that from an identity-work perspective, people are always active in shaping their identities – i.e., they have *agency* – whereas in the roles approach they tend to be passive – accepting their roles as given and something to be trained into. It's also important to note that from a critical perspective, identity-work is often a struggle as we try to deal with our own and others' interpretations of what we should be doing and who we are (Reedy, 2009; Warhurst, 2011). Let's take an example: you are a programme manager responsible for getting new products to market by coordinating a team of people from research and development, manufacturing, engineering and marketing, all of whom have different ideas about what your role should be. You have no authority over team members from other functions and the company's process management model doesn't clarify this. Your manager sees you as a 'facilitator and integrator', and you find yourself trying to figure out what this means by spending a fair amount of time talking to people, understanding team members' concerns and expectations, and building relationships to establish your credibility. In doing so, you are engaging in the struggle to shape your sense of identity.

### Managing is performative

Performativity is based on John L. Austin's (1962) idea that words are not just words, they *do* things and create action. For example, 'You are an average employee' or 'You are now promoted to human resource director', has an influence on how a person acts – in the latter example on the ways we expect HR directors to behave and talk.

Feminist philosopher Judith Butler has done much to develop the notion of performativity, particularly in relation to gender-identity. Let's look at some of her ideas because they pave the way for looking at performativity in a management context. In *Gender Trouble*, first published in 1990, Butler draws on Austin's notion that words do things to argue controversially that gender is performative: gender and identity do not exist per se, but are ongoing and open, created, maintained and refashioned in our desires, words, gestures, acts and in social discourse. We might have the illusion of a given and stable gender-identity, but it is an effect, a 'repeated stylization of the body, a set of repeated acts within a highly rigid regulatory frame that congeal over time to produce the appearance of substance, of a natural sort of being' (1990: 43–4). We learn to act and dress like men or women.

There is an extensive body of functionalist-based management scholarship carrying the assumption that theory informs practice by establishing a 'set of repeated acts' for managers, management students and management educators (see Chapter 1). But these theories are not just about actions and behaviour, they are also about language – creating accepted ways of talking (discourses with a small 'd'). Forbes Magazine[1] recently came up with the 45 most annoying and meaningless business phrases that management students learn and take into practice. This language is authoritative because it brings actions and identities into being and yet at the same time can conceal hidden meanings and implications. For example, 'empowering' often means giving employees more 'freedom', which means taking on additional responsibilities without any additional pay.

For Butler, gender and identity are performed and come into being through language: they are neither fixed nor free-floating but 'performatively constituted by the very "expressions" that are said to be its results' (1990: 33). Elizabeth Kelan (2013) looks at the performance of gender and the identity struggles of female managers and MBA students to 'appear professional'. She argues that dress plays an important role in becoming a manager and that this is easier for men than women, because women have to balance complying 'with a masculine script for leadership' and also 'be readable as women' (2013: 48), i.e., not appear too feminine or too masculine. Kelan's study draws on Butler's argument that gender and identity are political because they are constructed and performed with particular interests and goals in mind that privilege a masculine culture and identity and exclude others. But while Butler calls for subversion, Kelan uses media images of businesswomen (e.g., from the magazine *Management Today* and the TV programme *Sex in the City*) to help students reflect on identity issues and make judgements about how to position themselves as a manager. Studying social and organizational life through language, dress and other images is known as *semiotics*, which we'll explore further in Chapter 4.

Performativity, gender and identity politics are important concepts for managers to understand – because words not only *author* actions and construct the identities and behaviours they supposedly describe, they also give *authority* and power over others. How do words such as 'manager' and 'employee', and business school jargon such as 'Management by Walking About' construct the very behaviours and actions they supposedly describe? Gender, identity and 'management' are all located in a history of repeated practices and D/discourses that influence the way people act and interact. As we will see in the various Discourses of identity-work that follow, some authors see managers having little choice in selecting their identity, while others believe managers have a choice in challenging and constructing their identity.

We will now look at various D/discourses of identity and identity-work around being and becoming a manager, and will end by looking at the main theme of this book: that whether you are a CEO, a production, finance or marketing manager, *managing is a relational, reflexive and ethical practice*. In other words, managing is embedded in relationships with people, in what we say and do, and therefore we need to understand the crucial nature of language and our everyday communicative practices.

## Discourses of managerial identity-work

A review of the literature on the nature of managerial work and manager identities reveals a range of approaches, underpinned by assumptions from realism to social constructionism, determinism to free will, and coherence to fragmented and free-floating realities and identities. At the risk of oversimplifying, these approaches draw on the different assumptions of reality we discussed in the previous chapter and relate to whether the authors believe that:

- There is a real social reality out there that exists independently from us (*realism*) or we shape our social realities in our interactions and conversations (*social constructionism*).
- We can discover a universal and unified definition of managerial identity (*realism*) or that managerial identities are socially and/or linguistically constructed and therefore relative to time, place and personal experience (*social constructionism*).
- The manager is a passive instrument on which identity or cultural meanings are inscribed, or she or he exercises free will and interpretive choice in deciding what to do and who to be.

- Managerial identity is a social, an individual and/or a relational attribute.
- Managerial identities are coherent, contested or somewhere in-between.

Where you fall on these issues will influence not just how you think about management, but also how you manage and interact with employees. For example, a 'real' reality means that you probably expect people to conform and act in the right and rational way. Socially constructed realities mean working with people to understand different interpretations and perspectives and negotiate some shared sense of what might be happening. Table 1.1 highlighted some of the earlier studies, which tend to view identity from a realist, mainly passive, coherent and socially attributed or determined perspective. A number of contemporary studies have taken more of a constructed and contested view, discovering that even managers themselves find it difficult to define their identity and articulate what it is that they do (e.g., Sims, 2003; Thomas and Linstead, 2002). Tony Watson and Pauline Harris suggest this opaqueness means managers' identities are always emerging, and that management is a social process in which managers make 'their worlds at the same time as their worlds are making them' (1999: 238). Thus, identity-work is precarious and managers often feel insecure and vulnerable.

Let's have a look at some of the different ways of talking about and constructing managerial identities. I've summarized these in Figure 3.1.

## Managers as rational agents: real reality

> Ra·tion·al (adj): Able to think clearly and sensibly, because the mind is not impaired by physical or mental condition, violent emotion, or prejudice.[2]

As we have seen, the twentieth century was dominated by rational models situated within a realist perspective that attempted to define generalized characteristics of managerial work, managerial functions, activities, roles and competencies. These models helped systematize and legitimize management as a profession by bringing the logic of technical rationality, 'scientific' principles and objectivity to management – and also to behaviour in organizations. For example, early theories of motivation draw on the premise of 'rational economic man', a perfectly informed individual who makes choices based on weighing the costs and benefits of each course of action and who is motivated by money (recall Frederick Taylor's work). Management students also search for

**Figure 3.1**    Discourses of identity-work

rationality – wanting to know the right answer, the right way of doing something and how to get to the 'truth' … because to be rational is to be right … and to be right gives you power and legitimacy. This goes back to Max Weber's ([1924] 1947) argument that rational-legal authority is essential to bureaucracy – and bureaucracies should encompass rational systems of measurement and control.

Much of management practice, research and management education is based on the principle of rationality. Charles Kepner and Benjamin Tregoe (1965) published *The Rational Manager*, an influential text that identified a rational process of decision-making. There's now a

Kepner-Tregoe worldwide consulting organization offering solutions to human and organizational problems. This is achieved through the KT Way®, which focuses on reaching the right decision through rational thinking (with emotion and subjectivity removed), and a rational process of situational appraisal, problem analysis, decision analysis and potential problem (opportunity) analysis. As is typical of rational management, these processes are 'universally applicable and involve analytical thinking'.[3]

While this might sound very logical and acceptable, from a critical perspective we need to examine the ideas of rationality and rational managers more carefully. The pitfalls of rationality were brought sharply into focus in the recent UK Mid Staffordshire National Health Service (NHS) Foundation Trust scandal. A public inquiry was established to investigate high patient death rates and complaints about appalling patient care between 2005 and 2009. The 2013 Francis Report,[4] which makes harrowing reading, identified numerous problems including: poor leadership, a dysfunctional surgical group and management thinking dominated by financial control and statistical targets such as reducing waiting times. This led to a focus on the means (information systems, budgetary controls and performance management systems), rather than the ends (patient care and well-being). In the process, patients and employees were de-humanized and their experience ignored (remember the criticism of evidence-based management?). The report also condemns the Trust's culture of 'self-promotion rather than critical analysis and openness' (2013: 44) – an observation supporting the need for more reflexive managers.

So rationality is contested both conceptually and practically. If there *is* one rationality, then why do we have disagreement and conflict? Surely, we'd all come to the same conclusion and organizations would run perfectly – unless of course you have to deal with 'irrational' people who are not objective and make decisions based on value judgements! And yes, this statement is made tongue-in-cheek, because it raises the question, 'Whose rationality is the right one?' The contested nature of rationality can be seen in a 2008 article, 'How Apple got everything right by doing everything wrong', in which Kahney talks about CEO Steve Jobs' counter-rationality and includes the following quote: '"Steve proves that it's OK to be an asshole," says Guy Kawasaki, Apple's former chief evangelist. "I can't relate to the way he does things, but it's not his problem. It's mine. He just has a different OS."' I'm not advocating that managers be assholes – I'm merely pointing out that there's more than one 'operating system' or rationality. That what might seem perfectly rational to the manager making a decision, may seem irrational to the person implementing the decision.

In addition, rationality, as Gareth Morgan ([1986] 2006) points out, is political because managers use rationality to justify and achieve their own personal, work and career interests. Having worked in and with a number of organizations, experience tells me that on a day-to-day basis, organizations encompass many different rationalities. And maybe it's just me, but I have never been able to successfully apply the seven 'rational' principles of a more organized life, the ten steps to fitness, or the five stages to financial and/or career success because life is not that simple (or perhaps I'm just trying to rationalize my non-rationality?!).

Another major critique is that rationality carries a subtext of binary oppositions:

| | |
|---|---|
| Rational | Non-rational |
| Control | Chaos |
| Intellectual | Emotional |
| Neutral | Subjective |
| Mind | Body |
| Male | Female |

This goes back to French philosopher Derrida's work. He argues (1978) that words derive their meaning from their opposite, for example, good/bad, male/female, organization/disorganization. So when you use one term (e.g., rational), you are implicitly drawing on its opposite (non-rational). Think about the interrelationship of opposites when making a decision about an important issue – we may try to think about it rationally, but emotions, feelings about the people involved, and perhaps even a fear of being wrong, all play through that 'rational' decision.

Derrida also argues that we privilege one term over the other, for example, it's better to be rational than non-rational. The privileged term becomes an unquestioned norm against which we evaluate people, and which can favour one group or person over another. An example of the impact of this privileging process is the criteria used in performance evaluations and managerial competency models, such as 'objectively identifies problems' and 'calculates impact of actions' (see the Hay Group (2001) Manager Competency Model). What this means is that managers can use the term 'rational', intentionally or otherwise, to justify their interests and legitimate their authority, because being rational is good and right whereas being 'irrational' (or not subscribing to one particular version of rationality) is wrong. *Rationality is thus based on who has the power to decide what is rational* – an issue we'll explore further in Chapter 4.

## Managers as actors: performed realities

A contrasting Discourse to that of managers as rational agents is that of managers as actors. This draws on Erving Goffman's (1959, 1961, 1967) work on dramaturgy, the idea that we are all actors engaged in ongoing performances of the real. Within a dramaturgical perspective, identity is a *dramatic realization* of a social role, consistent with social norms and expectations, and organizations are social dramas or 'theatres' consisting of many different performances coordinated to achieve organizational goals. Managers are actors, acting out pre-existing performance scripts and roles (identities), managing performances and defining the roles and scripts of others. Individuals and teams cooperate in performances and follow routines: pre-established patterns of action. Many organizations now have corporate communication departments which stage elaborate productions such as annual general meetings, government press releases and product launches (see Biehl-Missal (2011) for examples of 'business as show business' performances). Goffman differentiates between frontstage and backstage performances. Let's say your organization is introducing a new information management system. Your frontstage performance will probably include meetings and presentations to employees, with an official script about the necessity and value of the new system. Backstage performances might include behind-the-scenes preparations and conversations with other managers about the problems of the new system and doubts about it ever working! So frontstage performances are about managing the impressions of others through appearance, actions, language, and so on. Simon Lewin and Scott Reeves (2011) found that interprofessional teamwork between doctors and nurses at a large UK teaching hospital occurred more often backstage than frontstage. Frontstage activities such as ward rounds were structured, task oriented and often brief, in order to give patients an impression of collaboration. Backstage performances, such as ad hoc hospital corridor conversations, were used for more in-depth and sometimes emotional discussions about patients and treatments. Indeed, Goffman says that any dissent should be relegated to backstage and that deviants from a frontstage norm are often marginalized.

So from a dramaturgical perspective, managers as actors see frontstage performances as strategic interactions where they deliberately act their identity to maintain a common audience perception. However, Goffman says that we present a *face* or *mask* (an image of oneself) in front of different audiences. For example, we might present the face to employees of 'I'm a good manager because I involve you in decisions', and the face of 'I make sure my employees toe the line' to our boss. Or we might present an image to avoid losing face when we make mistakes or fail (see

Helena Liu's 2010 study of leaders as 'failure framers' for examples). Ian Greener (2007) found within the UK National Health Service that senior managers collaborated in a face-saving performance to conceal the erosion of clinician power and allow them to believe they were still in charge. The senior managers achieved their agendas by paying deference to clinicians and getting their agreement on issues frontstage. This allowed the clinicians to believe they were still in charge, and yet they had to comply with the agreed decisions or they would lose face. So while the senior managers were acting out their identity within prescribed scripts, they were also improvising to achieve their agendas.

Managing in a dramaturgical context means creating a play (or a series of plays) with plots, various scenes and characters or roles for organizational members. Isn't this idea rather far-fetched? Maybe not – I put on my suit (costume) to come to work, I interact with people at work differently from the way I interact with friends and family (frontstage compared to backstage), I set goals and plans to achieve them (plots), talk to peers about how to present an idea or to members of my department about a change in work systems (scenes), create job descriptions and person specifications (character), etc. In Goffman's sense, managers are actors involved in *impression management*: presenting a positive social identity of being a credible manager who can successfully stage managerial performances. The relationship between impression management, language and identity was noted by one of my students:

> During my early days as a manager the one item I found most difficult was that of language. I pride myself on being an extremely honest person and truly believe in what DS [a guest speaker] told us, 'Without trust societies and economies fall apart.' My early observations of other leaders, was their tendency to use words that often seemed misleading. Instead of admitting to the mistake of over-hiring staff they would emphasize their frugalness in performing layoffs. Instead of confessing that they made a bad hire they would characterize the terminated manager as a disappointment to all senior management. In hindsight, these managers were choosing their words carefully, or framing, in an attempt to define a reality different to that I saw. I found it difficult to participate in what I considered dishonest games …

As well as performing a coherent frontstage performance, these managers were also engaged in face-saving, which caused a personal dilemma regarding conformity for my student who later found himself overlooked in a management reorganization.

Of course this raises the question as to whether managers who are good actors are being savvy manipulators and disingenuous in their relationships? From a managerialist perspective, impression management is just part of the repertoire of tools available to ensure the achievement of organizational goals. From a critical perspective it can be about faking emotion and identity (e.g., Tracy, 2000) as managers and employees find themselves required to act in ways they find stressful and humiliating – what Heather Höpfl (2002) calls performed hypocrisy. For example, for a short time my daughter had a job as a teller in a US bank. Her manager told her that she had to learn to smile more 'authentically' and to better project the 'WOW! factor' to customers, which Lauren felt meant being overly perky and inauthentic – something she just couldn't do!

For the rational manager, emotions are to be erased, masked or managed in organizational life. We rarely consider emotion on management courses and if we do it's often in a disembodied way as the characteristics of 'emotional intelligence' (something a manager needs to have). In my daughter's situation it was about *emotional labour*, being required to display – to act out – specific emotions on the job. Arlie Hochschild's 1983 study of Delta Airline flight attendants drew attention to emotional labour, the idea that emotions are turned into commodities from which the organization can profit. She found that flight attendants were required to 'love the job' and to smile. They were trained to manage and act out required emotions and also in anger-desensitization. Some attendants coped with the emotional requirements by separating their 'real' and 'fake' selves, but then had to deal with feelings that they were being insincere. So there are personal costs to emotional labour as employees and managers experience ethical dilemmas, emotional conflict and feelings of inauthenticity: Is this really who I am? Can I act the part and feel good about myself? These are struggles of identity and relationships: aesthetic labour diminishes spontaneity of feeling, genuine civility and concern, and can be perceived as calculated manipulation. To what extent is it morally acceptable to require employees to *be* in a particular way – because this form of labour is not just a performance, but relates to identity, emotions and our sense of self.

In contrast, Jenna Ward and Robert McMurray (2011) found that GP (doctor) receptionists learned to manage and suppress their emotions in various ways during the long, intense and often stressful periods they were dealing with patients. In this context, in contrast to the emotional excesses Hochschild's employees were expected to present, a degree of *emotional neutrality* was important in helping receptionists deal with the stress.

Does this indicate that managers need to be more reflexive about what they do and what they ask their employees to do?

## Managers of meaning: linguistically constructed realities

This Discourse addresses how managers create shared meanings and common definitions about situations that will then form the basis for action. It comes from a different tradition to that of Goffman's performance. Both relate to the notion that we construct our social realities in our interaction, but whereas Goffman sees performance as a collaborative, ritualistic, more-or-less prescribed and deliberate performance, managing meaning involves a greater degree of spontaneity, responsiveness to our surroundings and individuality, in the sense that our personal life history also influences our identity. The management of meaning tends to draw from Karl Weick's (1995) work on sensemaking and from a narrative and storytelling tradition. It also emphasizes the importance of language in shaping meaning and organizing action.

Let's begin with Weick, who over the last 30 years has done much to develop the notion of sensemaking in organizational life. Weick (2001) sees sensemaking as *committed interpretation* – people interpreting meanings and trying to define situations and justify their actions within a context, where social anchors and commitments influence action and where interactions create social commitments. For example, managers behave in ways towards employees because ... it's their role, their boss expects it, they've been trained to do so, the bottom line requires it ... and those actions create commitments both from themselves and others to act in a particular way. They shape meaning by picking up these social commitments and cues in situations to create (talk into being) a coherent story of events.

As managers talk, they are not only communicating and shaping meaning, they are also creating and maintaining culture, strategy and action. Boas Shamir (2007) talks about strategic leaders and managers shaping meaning around five key areas: the environment, performance, vision and goals, ways of achieving goals, and the organization's ability to progress towards goal achievement. They do so by shifting between plain talk and rhetoric – symbolic, poetic and emotional forms of speaking (Gowler and Legge, 1996). But managing meaning is also about identity-work, because in creating meaning, managers are invoking their own beliefs about who they are, their personal knowledge and intuition and acting to maintain their identity and others' perception of that identity. Let me illustrate these ideas with a brief excerpt from my conversation with the vice president of a US public utility (see Cunliffe, 2001: 363):

> My job has turned to high risk since deregulation – even though it is still highly regulated. Before it was real easy. Now I feel like Paul Revere's horse – it was the horse that ran from Charlestown to Lexington – Paul yelled – nobody remembers the horse! That's the way I feel! [laughter].

Notice the shift from plain talk about 'deregulation' to rhetoric (Paul Revere's horse): it was the rhetoric that connected and gave me a sense of how he felt about the situation and his identity. His rhetoric generated a much more powerful and empathetic response in me than if he had said, 'I get little recognition'. Rhetoric can therefore be powerful in shaping meaning.

Managers therefore manage meanings and influence others through their language and the way they talk. Thomas, Sargent and Hardy (2011) studied how managers negotiated meaning around a change initiative in a telecommunications company. They identified the communicative practices that occurred in meetings, for example, how managers used affirming statements to agree with alternative meanings proposed by others, and dismissing statements that rebuffed such meanings. They also tracked the strands or themes that emerged, changed and developed around particular issues in the discussion.

A number of authors have explored how managers make meaning through storytelling. Creating a story is seen as a way of shaping meaning about our experience, working out our identity and also shaping action. David Boje (e.g., 1991, 2008) has studied storytelling in organizations over a number of years. He argues that storytelling is a way for organizational members to create meanings about the past, present and future because stories provide some continuity with the past and also help fashion the future. There's a great example of this on YouTube, where a 28-year-old Steve Jobs 'performs' his 1983 Apple keynote speech, introduces the by now classic 1984 Macintosh advert and re-energizes a demotivated sales force.[5] It's well worth watching. Notice the music, the build-up of the story of a heroic Apple versus the monolithic IBM, the symbolism and rhetoric of the Mac TV advert, and the response of the audience. A masterful manager of meaning!

So good managers and good storytellers are able to create and tell stories about events, people and heroes as a means of connecting employees to organizational culture and practice. Stories are also ways of handling the hurt of organizational experience (Watson, 2001). Imagine the stories employees may tell to help them deal with layoffs, bullying or inequitable treatment. Managers often tell stories in their everyday conversations. I noticed in one of my conversations with a vice president of a health care organization that he told a lot of stories (Cunliffe, 2001: 365). When I asked him to explain something, he often told a story. When I commented on this, he responded:

Mike:    and I do a lot of that. For me probably the most effective way in dialogue is to tell stories and use analogies and to make pictures ...

Ann:     ... it can be very persuasive ...

Mike:    Yes, [...] by native style I'm much more a storyteller. Matter of fact sometimes for presentations I've written fables and presented ... a particular Board of Directors – I remember we were struggling with an issue about strategy and where do we go, and they had a very difficult time seeing themselves in the picture – right? – and what they were causing to happen in the organization. And so I wrote this about 6–8 page fable and read it at the board meeting, about the Middle Ages, and likened our organization to a marauding band that had to support itself off the land at the same time it was trying to ... and they got it! They could find themselves! And it was very helpful.

Ann:     Did they make those connections with themselves?

Mike:    Oh yes, it wasn't subtle [laughter]. It just moved it out into a safer context in which for them to see themselves, for them to say this is what we're doing. Is this a problem we're causing ...?

So in this example, the vice president sees his identity as a natural storyteller and uses stories deliberately to shape meaning and actions of his board of directors in a very different way.

David Sims (2008) suggests that managers engage in identity-work by narrating themselves as the main character in a coherent narrative or story. For example, a colleague might ask us why we made a decision or acted in a particular way, so we explain by pulling together and connecting what we see as all the events, reasons, feelings, who said what to whom, what we did and why, etc., to *narrate* or plot a story and at the same time establish our credibility as a manager. Sims examines five stories he told over a period of time when re-shaping his identity from an academic to becoming a manager: stories of gaining experience, cleaning the stables, creating bliss, entrapment and life after death. This always involves a degree of uncertainty because we are learning as we go along, we try out stories that may be contested or ignored by others, and we may fantasize new identities based on observations of how other managers or fictitious characters act. Such characters can be seen in TV programmes such as *Mad Men* – about macho and ambitious executives in a fictional US advertising agency – or *The Thick of It* – centring around the aggressive and manipulative Malcolm Tucker, director of communications at the fictitious UK Department of Social Affairs and Citizenship. But we also have reality TV shows such as *Undercover Boss* (franchised across many countries) where the owner of a business takes on the undercover identity of an entry-level employee usually to learn to become a better manager – a media-based example of identity-work at play?!

Sims (2003) argues that middle managers are particularly vulnerable when engaging in identity-work because they are in career transition and have to deal with the differing expectations of senior management and subordinates – and both expect 'good' stories that are meaningful and will hold their attention. They often find themselves having to tell stories to subordinates that they themselves do not believe, or stories that later may be publicly discredited by senior management. So they are constantly trying to save face and maintain their sense of identity.

To summarize, managing meaning is about managers shaping understanding and creating stories to organize action and help them enact and work out their identity in their talk and interactions with others. This means creating stories and characters that are plausible and resonate with others. Managing meaning is not performing a script (as in managers as actors), but involves a 'willingness to forgo planning and rehearsing in favor of acting in real time' (Weick, 2001: 299). For Weick, if we are overly concerned with technique and scripts, then we are often poor improvisers, and because managers have to deal with ambiguities, uncertainties, contradictions and discontinuities, they need to learn to improvise. It's also important to note a major difference between the Discourses of managers of meaning and managers as rational agents. Instead of privileging one meaning (the right one) and one side of a binary opposition (i.e., rational versus non-rational), managers of meaning recognize that meaning-making is ongoing, subject to multiple interpretations and the interplay of binary oppositions, in that managers focus both ends of the binary, for example, resilience and routine.

### Managers as discursive subjectivities: performativity and fragmented realities

Let's begin with what is meant by 'discursive subjectivities'. This perspective draws on poststructuralist thought, which addresses how knowledge, institutional structures and language systems (Discourse with a capital 'D') and language and talk (discourse with a small 'd') shape realities and regulate what is seen as 'normal'. So scholars taking a D/discursive approach study the relationship between language, social action and social theory. Knowledge plays a disciplining role in this process because it consists of unconscious rules and practices that determine: what is 'good' knowledge; what are 'good' standards for judgement; who are experts; and therefore who can control meaning and speak for others. These practices are riddled with power, because they privilege particular ideologies, social structures, institutional practices and groups over others (Foucault, 1970, 1972). In terms of management, this means examining how talk, written text, physical and symbolic artifacts, and broader social, historical, economic and ideological forces shape management theory, practice and identity.

As I outlined in Chapter 1, many poststructural studies draw on the work of Michel Foucault (1980, 1988), who argued that the subject (identity) is the product of various discourses and forms of knowledge. In Foucauldian terms, D/discourse constructs and categorizes the individual and is inscribed on our bodies – structuring our behaviour, desires and ways of talking. This turns us into a *subjectivity*, a site where D/discourses of power and control meet and organize identity, and in the process create conflict by subjecting us to forces and practices with which we may disagree and may either conform or try to resist. Identity – subjectivity – is therefore inscribed, image-driven, contradictory, fragmented, elusive and power-ridden.

There are at least two distinctions in the managers as discursive subjectivities Discourse from the previous ones. First, this Discourse is not about identity-work, but *identity regulation* – managers as discursive subjectivities are not actively involved in creating their own identity, but subject to discursive, linguistic and structural forces over which they have no control. Second, managerial subjectivity is performative, but in a different sense from Goffman's performance. In *Bodies That Matter* (1993), Judith Butler differentiates the two: performing is a conscious performance of a ritual, while performativity is concealed in performance and is discursive – a powerful form of speech that produces actions and an *unconscious* reiteration of a norm or social category.

Subjectivities are also multiple and fragmented as different D/discourses create competing pressures. Alison Pullen (2006) examines the subjective identities of middle managers within broader social discourses and gendered organizational discourses, arguing that managers' identities are sites of negotiation and contestation. This issue of contestation is highlighted in Darren McCabe's (2008) study of a UK bank. Employees and managers struggled with contradictory organizational Discourses of the 'enterprise self', as they were required to focus on the customer, use initiative, be a teamworker and take responsibility for their actions, yet also be a submissive, self-shackled by cost controls, individual evaluation systems and autocratic decisions.

Let's take a hypothetical example to see how managers can be viewed as discursive subjectivities:

You work in XL as a middle manager. The company currently stresses transformational leadership, performance metrics, organizational agility and creative partnering, as expressed in the company value statement. These are four significant organizational discourses reinforced by the CEO's speeches to the media, and in meetings with senior managers and middle managers (discourse). You have been through programmes training you to be visionary, charismatic and proactive; how to control department costs and performance through measurement; how to monitor and adapt quickly to technological advancements and market changes; and how to be more flexible in working across department boundaries to improve productivity and quality. Yet managers are evaluated and rewarded individually on whether their department is under budget, and whether they have met production targets on time. Five years ago you had the authority to do what it took to make something happen, but now you have to get pre-approval for anything that involves expenditure over £500, and the process can take anything from six months to a year depending on the amount of justification required by senior management ...

The four organizational Discourses, along with discursive practices such as training, appraisal and information systems, regulate the identities of managers by requiring specific actions and behaviours. As the manager, you have to make choices about what to do and which identity to take at any particular moment in time: an inspirer of others, an enforcer of performance standards for individual employees, an innovator who is subject to close controls, and a collaborator with others as and when needed. You are frustrated trying to balance the demands of each, by trying to be proactive while feeling like a puppet because you have no authority and spend your time producing statistics. You try to remain positive with your staff, while remaining distant from your boss who trots out the company line. Most middle managers in your organization just keep their heads down and focus on meeting short-term goals, while complaining to each other about conflicting demands. Some are deliberately uncooperative, and refuse to attend any more training sessions. You feel torn in different directions and struggle to find a sense of coherence, and find yourself becoming less and less committed to the organization ...

This example attempts to show how managers can be constructed as multiple and fragmented subjectivities – as effects of D/discursive processes, tossed between contested meanings and shifting fields of power, which they accept – i.e., passive dupes of identity regulation. It also illustrates that some managers may actively subordinate themselves to the demands in order to be rewarded – or may passively resist by opting out.

There are those who argue that this way of thinking about the identity of managers is overly pessimistic. Are we just products of external forces? Can we be creative in resisting imposed identities? Or are we somewhere in-between as simultaneously consentors and resisters? Russell Warhurst (2011) offers a more optimistic reading of managerial identity than the 'discursively deceived demons' (2011: 275) conceived of by the identity regulation model, finding MBA students in his study 'actively embracing identity formation opportunities' (2011: 270) and questioning managerial decisions they accepted previously. Mary Phillips and Deborah Knowles (2012) also believe that there are alternative performativities. They use Butler's ideas to argue that entrepreneurial subjectivities are performatively constructed through 'repeated acts' and dominant discourses that are masculine, e.g., entrepreneurs are 'self-made men'. Women entrepreneurs are often subject to masculine discourses (be aggressive, decisive, self-confident) that make them invisible and their life difficult if they try to adopt male norms because they are seen as lacking 'male' credibility. The other possibility is that women can 'do' (perform) entrepreneurship differently from this male discourse. Viewing managers as discursive subjectivities can offer a different way of thinking about what, or who, managers are and how they relate to their surroundings.

## Relational and reflexive managers: questioning socially constructed realities

The corporate leaders we interviewed indeed produced an extensive list of qualities they desired in future recruits, but almost none involved functional or technical knowledge. Rather, virtually all their requirements could be summed up as follows: the need for more thoughtful, more aware, more sensitive, more flexible, more adaptive managers, capable of being moulded and developed into global executives. (Barker, 2010: 59)

I begin with this quote from a recent formal review of London Business School's MBA programme because it illustrates the need for reflexivity and relationality – for managers to be more thoughtful and sensitive. I would, however, question the idea that we can and should 'mould' people – an issue we'll address in the next chapter. I believe the important question is: *What might such 'thoughtfulness' look like?*

Relational and reflexive managers are people who recognize that they, along with others, 'author' or shape social and organizational realities (culture, policies, structure and practices, etc.) in everyday conversations and interactions. In doing so, they accept responsibility for creating those shared realities and question how their assumptions and actions impact how people experience those realities. This Discourse therefore embraces social constructionist assumptions and a critical approach by examining what we are taking for granted when interacting with and managing others ... which is what much of this book is about.

A social constructionist approach to managing was first proposed by John Shotter (1993), who argued that managers are 'authors' shaping organizational realities from a 'chaotic welter of impressions', and in doing so try to negotiate some kind of shared meaning and create new possibilities for coordinating actions and moving forward. Indeed, when you ask managers about their experience, they rarely talk about structures, roles, scripts or performances, but about how they are continually trying to make sense of ill-defined aspects of their work: about feeling pushed or pulled in different directions, the dilemmas they face in terms of who they are and what to say or do. One of my interests over the last 15 years or so has been to develop this idea and explore what relationality and reflexivity means in practice for leading, managing and designing organizations (e.g., Cunliffe, 2001, 2009; Shotter and Cunliffe, 2002).

The Discourse of relational managers draws on the alternative ways of understanding language, reality and communication that we discussed in Chapter 2. Organizational realities and identity-work occur in our conversations and relationships with others: in what we say, *how* we say it and how we interact with others. This differs from the Discourses of managers as actors and managers of meaning because it goes beyond performing roles and scripts, beyond the words used by a manager, to the *living conversations* (Bakhtin, 1986) and dialogue *between* people. In other words, relational managers assume that we do not live, act and talk in isolation, we are always in relation to others whether they are present or not. We create meaning, action and try to shape our identities *with others in relationally-responsive and dialogic interaction*. However, because managers have influence, they play a crucial role in authoring these relationships. These ideas re-vision man*aging* as a continually emerging, embodied and responsive practice, *a way of being and relating* – rather than the conventional view of manage*ment* as a series of disembodied activities or roles within an already existing reality.

Managing is therefore about who we are, because our actions, our ways of making sense and shaping our world are not separate from us, they do not stem from a detached knowledge of the world, but are intimately linked to who we are, what we feel and say, and how we engage with our surroundings. We are therefore always engaged in identity-work, whether or not we realize it.

Where does reflexivity come in? Reflexivity recognizes that talk and action, self and others, are interwoven and therefore it's important for managers to *question how* they relate with others. This means thinking about the assumptions we hold about people and how such assumptions influence the way people may respond, understanding how others may view the world and creating opportunities for open dialogue. This was underscored by one of my EMBA students, who commented:

> I think the point is that it is always about how you are affecting other people. It always has been. The problem is that we are not aware of the importance of focusing on how we interact with others. We do not stop to consider how we affect others and how our actions could result in showing disrespect for their values. By considering people as a means of accomplishing tasks that need to be completed, you are essentially stripping them of their 'humanness'. You are treating them as a commodity, a means to an end.

While many management education programmes emphasize the need for reflection, few move towards what I believe is fundamental to managing organizations in responsive, responsible and ethical ways – *reflexivity*. So let me begin by explaining the difference between reflection and reflexivity.

Have you ever completed a personality or a management style questionnaire? If so, then this was used as a tool to help you reflect on your personality type and become a better person and/or choose an appropriate style. These questionnaires categorize you in comparison to types or norms that are deemed to exist. For example, using the Myers Briggs personality types you could be an ISTJ (introvert, sensing, thinking, judging) person, and knowing this can help you choose the best career. *Reflection* – whether about personality, people, management or organizational problems – is based on a realist view of the world as consisting of concrete objects and patterns of behaviour that we can measure, categorize and develop a theory or model to explain. Reflection is also associated with assumptions of a person as a rational being with an inner consciousness, who can think logically, analytically and in an objective way. Indeed, John Dewey (1910), one of the best-known authors in this field, argued that reflection and a logically-trained mind are key to becoming an educated person. This was further reinforced by Donald Schön (1983), who argued that competent professionals engage in reflective practice as a means of dealing with complex and uncertain situations. They do so by *reflecting-in-action*, engaging in a reflective conversation and constructing an understanding of the situation using a repertoire of personal experience and situational knowledge. This reflective conversation involves framing and reframing the problem, finding alternatives and judging the possible impact of alternative courses of action. Reflection means standing back and looking at a situation in a logical way.

Reflexivity draws on social constructionism to emphasize our responsibility for shaping our world. It goes deeper than reflection by interrogating what we might be taking for granted as we interact with other people, try to make sense of our world and create knowledge. So managers as reflexive authors routinely engage in a more critical and questioning stance, as seen in the comment below from one of my EMBA students:

> I have become more critical of my goals and the means of attaining them. This has opened me up to a deeper examination of the truths/ assumptions that I've held which has led to many questions, the pursuit of these questions – not necessarily their answers – are taking me to a next level of understanding.

Elsewhere (Cunliffe, 2003, 2009), I've suggested that reflexivity is situated in constructionist and deconstructionist approaches, and that the former can be linked to self-reflexivity, the latter to critically-reflexive practice. Table 3.1 summarizes the main assumptions of each approach.

As relational and reflexive authors, managers engage in both. But what does this mean? Being *self-reflexive* means accepting our responsibility for shaping our world: questioning our ways of being, relating and acting and thinking about how, in our living conversation with others, our assumptions, words and responses influence meaning and help shape organizational 'realities' and identities. In doing so, we question the limitations of our assumptions and our sensemaking; whether we respond defensively or openly to people; and the multiplicity of meanings and

**Table 3.1**  Assumptions underlying reflexivity

| Self-Reflexivity | Critical-Reflexivity |
|---|---|
| *Social and Organizational Realities*: | *Social and Organizational Realities*: |
| Emerge in everyday conversational activities. | Constructed through discursive and non-discursive practices. |
| 'Realities' are shaped and maintained in language and talk. | 'Realities' are fragmented, fleeting and contested. |
| Organizations are language communities and/or communities of social practices. | Organizations are discursively constructed sites of power, discipline, normalization, marginalization and resistance. |
| *Self*: | *Self*: |
| Selves and identities are shaped in everyday interaction. | A subject constructed and normalized through discursive practices. |
| *Language*: | *Language*: |
| What we say, and how we say it, shapes meaning and creates and reproduces social realities. | The separation of words and objects. Meaning is constantly deferred and constructed through binary oppositions. |
| *Knowledge*: | *Knowledge*: |
| An implicit and indexical knowing, sensemaking within contexts, knowledge as interpretation and insight. | A political process of the production of temporary texts, 'facts' and 'truths', and the consumption of such texts. |
| *Self-Reflexivity*: | *Critical-Reflexivity*: |
| Exposing the situated, tentative and provisional nature of our social and organizational realities and knowledge. | Destabilizing and deconstructing truths, ideologies, language, overarching narratives, single meanings, authority and disciplinary practices. |
| Exploring how we constitute our social and organizational experience and identities in everyday interaction. | Revealing and interrogating assumptions that privilege particular groups. |
| Exploring multiple meanings and interpretations. | |

Source: after Cunliffe (2009)

voices we may or may not hear in our relationships and interactions with others. Being self-reflexive forms a basis for exploring how we may personally act in responsible and ethical ways.

*Critical-reflexivity* draws from critical theory, poststructural and postmodern commitments to unsettle the assumptions underlying theoretical,

ideological and organizational positions and practices. This means compli-
cating rather than simplifying, questioning rather than answering or
accepting, looking for paradoxes and contradictions rather than order and
patterns, thinking about what lies unsaid as well as what is said, and recognizing multiple perspectives rather than imposing an ideology or worldview. As critically-reflexive authors, managers aim to create more critical,
open dialogue and more responsive and ethical organizations, by:

- Examining assumptions of rationality underlying decisions.
- Engaging in debate about the purpose, practices and impact of organizations (profit, community and environmental well-being, etc.).
- Questioning 'normal' taken-for-granted strategies, policies, programmes and organizational practices as a basis for understanding
  how and why these practices might impact people and exclude them
  from active participation in organizational life ...

Critical-reflexivity involves questioning and turning ideas and assumptions back on themselves, which raises another aspect of Derrida's
work – that of *deconstruction*. Deconstruction is a way of reading
texts to reveal underlying assumptions, contradictions and how they
might privilege one truth or position over another. The TV 'mockumen-
tary', *The Office*, is an interesting example of a media deconstruction
and examination of managerial identities, 'rationality' and organizational culture. The programme reflexively draws attention to inappropriate and exaggerated management behaviours and practices – and
how employees resist these – by poking fun at them.

Joanne Martin (1990) brought deconstruction into the realm of
Organization Studies when she deconstructed a story told by the CEO
of a multinational corporation to illustrate the company's concern for
women. The story centred around a pregnant female employee who
arranged her Caesarean section around the launch of a new product she
had been involved in developing. The company provided a closed-circuit
television by her bed so she could watch the launch event. Martin provided alternative readings, one of which reframed the story as a male
employee, in the same situation, undergoing heart by-pass surgery. She
argued that in both cases, the action illustrated a breach of the public
(work) and private (personal life) divide, but in counterposing the two
stories, the Caesarean example illustrated not a humanistic concern for
the well-being of women, but a desire to maintain work productivity.

While deconstruction might seem like an academic and pointless linguistic exercise, I believe it is important to managers because deconstructing organizational texts such as policy documents, mission and media
statements, emails, and management systems and actions, can sensitize us

to hidden assumptions, silenced voices, to who or what is privileged, to alternative interpretations and to the consequences for organizational practices – intended or otherwise. Deconstruction can also help us raise a most critical question for managers: *Could what seems to me to be the 'reality' of the present situation be otherwise? Are there unnoticed openings for new possibilities and for taking a new direction?*

Relational managers therefore accept responsibility for their part in shaping organizational realities by engaging in a critical and self-reflexive questioning of what they, and others, are taking for granted. This means questioning not just the means, but also the ends – the impact. The news has been full of examples of what can happen when organization policies and practices based purely on the bottom line remain unquestioned. One such example is the UK's PPI scandal. PPI, payment protection insurance, was designed to help customers repay loans and debts in the event of job loss, illness, etc. This seems like a good idea because it offers protection for both customers and the bank. However, banks began to impose high sales targets on their staff to 'encourage' them to sell PPI to customers. If targets were not reached, penalties were imposed on individuals and branches. Employees were therefore pressured into selling – and mis-selling – insurance. Banks are now required to compensate customers who were forced into buying PPI. Perhaps if those who imposed the targets questioned the underlying motives – to maximize profit and increase efficiency – and considered the potential impact on staff and customers, they might have taken a more judicious approach. The point is that self- and critical-reflexivity are crucially tied to ethical management and leadership.

I often find when discussing the relevance of reflexivity with managers that their initial response is: we can't question everything all of the time or we'd *never* get anything done! I agree. It's about knowing what's important to question, and being aware of how we relate to others. As one manager in my EMBA course wrote:

> ... by caring, by empathizing, by questioning the assumptions behind systems, and by keeping an eye on what is truly important. That's a challenge for me. My experience, in 25 years at ___ Corporation, is that many of those systems have contributed to the success of one of the most successful companies in US history. But there *are* two ends of the 'manage' spectrum ... (Cunliffe, 2001): mana*ging* and manag*ement*. Mana*ging* is a way of being and relating – a continually emerging, embodied practice. Manag*ement* is a series of disembodied activities. And balancing the two, I believe, is critical: just as it is in the implementation of any philosophy, system or habit. A leader can spend too much time on

facts and details, concrete steps of implementation, HR policies and procedures and the like. A leader can also overly focus on being philosophic and questioning – to the neglect of proven leadership tools, principles and techniques as taught by the likes of Peter Drucker and Henry Mintzberg. So maintaining a balance is important...

To summarize, relational and reflexive managers see social and organizational life as emergent, socially constructed and inherently ideological and political. They challenge taken-for-granted organizational practices and, in doing so, emphasize their responsibility for managing in more responsive ways and helping shape new, more collaborative and inclusive forms of reality.[6]

## Summary

The purpose of this chapter is to highlight different Discourses of management, of which the more contemporary ones focus on the idea of managers as always engaged in identity-work. As such, one is always *becoming a manager*. Foundational ways of framing management as rational and neutral both legitimate and constrain managerial action and normalize identities. And even though the Discourse of managers as discursive subjectivities challenges the legitimation of management, its focus on identity regulation doesn't leave managers much option for change. In contrast, the Discourses of managers of meaning and relational managers offer not only a different way of thinking about who managers are, but also a different way of *doing and being* a manager.

I also highlight that whether we are managers or employees, we cannot separate ourselves and our relationships with others from our work. What we do, how we act and how we think about our work, how we interact with others, is closely tied with our emotions and our identity – with who we are. Many of the managers' and students' comments I include throughout the book are statements of identity-work: of emotional struggles at an individual or a collective level. The relationship between emotion and identity at work is a crucial one for managers to understand, but one that's often ignored.

Finally, I want to argue that rather than uncritically reproducing fixed representations of management and management identities, reflexive managers seek various conceptualizations and critiques of management as a means of exploring possibilities and rethinking how they would like organizations and management to be. We'll explore this in more depth in the following chapter.

## Notes

1. www.forbes.com/sites/groupthink/2012/01/26/the-most-annoying-pretentious-and-useless-business-jargon/ (accessed 4 September 2013).
2. *Encarta World English Dictionary*.
3. See the Kepner-Tregoe website, www.kepner-tregoe.com/knowledge-center/articles/developing-a-thinking-organization-part-ii (accessed 13 September 2013).
4. See the executive summary at: www.midstaffspublicinquiry.com/sites/default/files/report/Executive%20summary.pdf (accessed 4 September 2013).
5. www.youtube.com/watch?v=lSiQA6KKyJo (accessed 4 September 2013).
6. See Cunliffe (2009) for further discussion.

# 4

# Managing Culture – Managing Hearts, Minds and Souls

## Or ... Obversion, Subversion and Diversion

If you pick up a book on management, organization theory or organizational behaviour, there's a good chance it will include something about organizational culture: the values, practices, stories, heroes and management style of an organization. Originally the purview of anthropologists who went out into the field to study the beliefs, customs and ways of living of indigenous populations in distant primitive societies, culture became a key area of concern in Organization Studies in the 1980s. Organizational ethnographers began studying culture by spending time in organizations observing meetings and talking to employees to identify common assumptions, values and practices that influence organizational performance. Organizational culture became 'big business' as managers began to see it as a key determinant of organizational performance and competitiveness, because managing culture is about managing an organization's image with external and internal stakeholders, aligning individual goals with organizational goals, individual actions and identities with organizational requirements, and motivating people. However, as we will see, from a critical perspective culture can be insidious because it is also about power and control: about managing identities and the hearts, minds, bodies and souls of people.

I also want to point out that while culture is often associated with the identity or image of the organization, it simultaneously influences and is influenced by the identity-work of managers and employees, i.e., culture is not some*thing* that is external to us, but socially constructed and maintained in our interactions and conversations.

In this chapter, we will take a critical view of managing organizational culture by examining what could be termed the 'dark side' of culture:

- How culture can be viewed as a 'cult' in which employees are manipulated and marginalized in intended and unintended ways in the pursuit of excellence.

- How culture is dialectical: about both conformity and difference, control and resistance, power and empowerment, etc.
- How identity struggles are tied up with the experience and enactment of organizational culture.

It's important to question these taken-for-granted aspects of organizational culture as a means of understanding how organizational members might experience culture in different ways. Can we do anything about this 'dark side'? I believe so – if relational and reflexive managers begin to think about organizations as *communities of difference*, they may act to create more ethical and responsive organizations. So we'll look at some possibilities for change.

## The cult of culture

> Organizational culture: 'the shared view of reality, and the collective belief and value systems reflected in a consistent pattern of behaviors among participants'. (Jassawalla and Sashittal, 2002: 43)

> Cult: 'Obsessive, especially faddish, devotion to or veneration for a person, *principle, or thing*'.[1]

Why might culture be a 'cult'? Cults are usually viewed as characterized by strong beliefs, dedication to a particular ideology and ritualistic practices, and are often seen in a pejorative way if they are harmful to people. You may be wondering how this can possibly apply to business organizations … and yet notice some similarities between the two definitions above. Perhaps the most shocking examples of the 'cult' of culture are those relating to the financial crisis. Why do bank employees engage in risky, unethical and even illegal behaviour? Presumably they are normal people like us, who if asked whether they would ever do anything illegal would say, 'No, of course not!'. One such example is the Banca Monte dei Paschi di Siena (MPS), Italy's third largest and the world's oldest bank. Founded in 1472, it had a reputation for being solid and conservative, yet is now undergoing an inquiry into alleged fraud and corruption associated with market manipulation, money laundering and the obstruction of regulators. In 2012 MPS posted a €3.2 billion loss. In 2013 the chief finance officer was jailed and the chief communications officer apparently committed suicide.

However, the classic example is Enron. As a *Time* magazine article stated in February 2002 after the company filed Chapter 11 bankruptcy:

It was Skilling [the CEO] who provided the strategic vision behind Enron, who transformed its old gas-pipeline culture into a swaggering, rule-breaking, dealmaking cult that ultimately mislaid its analytical skills and perhaps its moral compass. Skilling, a Harvard M.B.A. and former McKinsey & Co. consultant, had a high-wattage intellect that always impressed. Even when he was a student, people who met him knew he would do something big.[2]

They perhaps didn't realize how big! Skilling was convicted for fraud, conspiracy, insider trading and lying to auditors, and was sentenced to 24 years in jail in 2006. The Enron corporate *cult*ure was one of 'creative' accounting, aggressive risk-taking and a feeling of invulnerability, where subsidiary companies were established with names inspired by *Star Wars* and *Jurassic Park* characters such as Raptor and Chewco. Imagine how difficult it was to go against the norm. It required moral courage to be the one person to defy orders or question unethical and (in this case) illegal action.

Why do such scandals occur? In the MPS case, poor management, a lack of supervision and politics are proposed to be the main causes. In relation to the Libor scandal (see Chapter 5), Vince Cable, UK Secretary of State for Business, Innovation and Skills, stated it was a banking culture of incompetence, corruption and greed.[3] Mark Stein (2011) argues that deeper and more insidious processes are at play in recent financial scandals. Drawing on a psychoanalytical perspective he argues that *manic cultures* have developed in which four key processes influence the behaviour of leaders, managers and organizational members:

1. Denial – problems and vulnerabilities are identified but not taken seriously.
2. Omnipotence – members of the organization feel all-powerful and infallible.
3. Triumphalism – a need to demonstrate superiority regardless of the consequences.
4. Over-activity – in which evidence of problems is destroyed and warnings and critics are attacked.

Stein further argues that leaders and managers may engage in *manic denial*, in which problems are seen as provocations to take even 'more extreme risks' (2011: 183). You may be getting a sense of how organizational cultures may be not too far removed from cults!

Let's begin to take a critical look at some of the taken-for-granted aspects of organizational culture and the kinds of issues that managers need to think about in more reflexive, relational and ethical ways. We'll begin by looking at whether organizational culture is about management, manipulation or both.

## Managing or manipulating culture?

If you study culture from a mainstream Management Studies perspective, you will come across the work of Edgar Schein. His 1985 model of the three levels of organizational culture – with *assumptions* at the taken-for-granted and deepest level, *values* at the next more accessible level, and finally *artifacts* at the most visible level – has formed the basis for many studies of organizational culture. But one of the precipitating factors in connecting academic with practitioner interest in culture was the advent of Tom Peters and Robert Waterman's 1982 best-selling book, *In Search of Excellence*, which identified the cultural attributes of successful organizations such as IBM and McDonalds. Tom Peters became a 'management guru', presenting his ideas around the world in more books, in videos, and countless seminars and televised national and worldwide conferences in the almost evangelical fervour of companies to reproduce cultures of 'excellence'. Many books, both academic and popular press, followed. In academic terms this is known as *mimetic isomorphism* – modelling the practices, values and behaviours of other organizations.

Managers wanted to know how to design high-performing 'excellent' companies and create committed and highly motivated employees by managing culture. So the 1980s and 1990s saw the advent of mission and vision statements, the identification of core values (service excellence, quality, etc.), buzzwords such as empowerment and autonomy, catchy phrases ('There's no "I" in "Team"'; 'Go for the Low-hanging Fruit'), and images such as the Nike logo. These cultural texts and artifacts are connected with the Discourses of managers as actors and managers of meaning, defining reality by managing frontstage performances, creating heroic images, symbols and stories, framing language and speaking rhetorically to manage the behaviour and performance of employees. Culture management is a key element of the managerialization and professionalization of management and from a realist and functionalist perspective is about creating homogeneity and a clear direction of effort. Many organizations give employees vision statements on credit card size cards that they can keep in their pocket as a constant reminder.

Why might this be problematic? Critical Management Studies scholars question the right of managers to manage the work performance of employees, arguing that managing is also about the hearts, minds and souls of employees; and that culture management is a form of social engineering (a large scale influencing of groups of people), of manipulation, and should therefore be open to destabilization and critique. One such critique is Rick Chapman's (2006) counter-*culture* book, *In Search of Stupidity: Over 20 Years of High-Tech Marketing Disasters*. In contrast to the 'excellence' literature, Chapman looks at how companies fail as they continue to make the same mistakes!

In his ethnographic study of culture in a US engineering company, Gideon Kunda found that 'management pays a great deal of attention to developing, articulating, and disseminating the organizational ideology for internal consumption' (1992: 218). Senior managers 'engineered' culture – the company ideology or official version of reality – through presentations, vision statements, work manuals, etc. But culture management isn't just about socializing employees to carry out their work and behave in specific ways, it's also about shaping employee identity in the corporate image. Indeed, many critically oriented studies of culture argue that organizational culture is an insidious form of manipulation designed to control the hearts, minds, bodies and souls of employees. Let's take a number of Microsoft's company values as an example: 'A passion for technology, respectful and open, accountable, honest and with integrity, self-critical, and eager to take on big challenges'.[4] We might not quibble with these values per se, but they raise an interesting question: Am I being manipulated if, as an employee, I have to be passionate (or at least display passion) about my work? What identity struggles do I find myself dealing with in trying to portray these characteristics? They may mean I'm required to think, feel and behave in ways which are stressful because they are not 'me' … but if I'm going to be evaluated and rewarded based on the degree to which I'm 'passionate', what do I do? Okay, this might seem cynical, but thinking about this reflexively suggests that managing culture could be perceived as a cult concerned with controlling the thoughts, desires and experiences of organizational members.

So culture is about the identity of the organization *and* the identity-work of employees. As Kunda argues, the organizational self is not an autonomous self, but is subject to normative controls (organizational norms and values) aimed at eliminating the fragmentation, contradiction and struggle for meaning and identity inherent to organizational life. He found that while most of the employees in the organization seemingly accepted the culture, they were at the same time wary and often cynical about it. Employees experienced *interpretive struggles* over expectations, and deviants were silenced, marginalized or became non-persons by being moved out of the organization or to less meaningful or influential jobs. Thus, your identity as an employee is a 'managed' identity, subject to control by those in power. The idea of managed identities brings to mind the experience of a student of mine who had a six-month internship in a sales company. The company had regular monthly review meetings at which each person's targets and actual sales for the period were announced. Those who exceeded their target were greeted with wild applause, those who hadn't with boos. Many of the sales staff lived in the same apartment complex and socialized as a group. Despite being offered a permanent job with a great salary, she ended up taking a less well-paid position because she felt uncomfortable with the normative demands and the pressures to conform – not just at work but also spilling over into the personal lives of employees. She was unwilling to participate, saying, 'It's just not who I am'. This raises an interesting question about how willing we are to conform to cultural norms that we do not agree with.

Even anthropologists are not immune from the charges of the manipulation of culture. In 2000, a controversy exploded over a well-known 1960s study of the Venezuelan Yanomami Indians. Allegations were made about culture manipulation, sexual misconduct, unethical experimentation, the staging of fake villages and the creation of conflict for the purpose of filming the supposedly natural fierce behaviours of the Yanomami people.[5] You might think that manipulating people and staging culture has nothing to do with organizations – but recall how the US energy company Enron managed to hide billions of dollars of debt and operating losses by creating fake partnerships and a fake trading room (complete with ringing phones and family photos on desks) where employees pretended to buy and sell energy contracts during a credit-rating visit from Wall Street analysts.[6] This might seem an extreme example, but such frontstage performances do occur in many organizations, not necessarily with the intention of being deliberately fraudulent, but with the purpose of managing impressions, which in Goffman's terms can be both deliberate and habitual. I'm reminded of the numerous planning meetings and rehearsals I've attended over the years, as part of the preparation for performances deemed necessary for business school accreditation visits!

This may leave us with rather a dark and cynical view of managers as manipulators of culture and people. It's not meant to be so. What these ideas offer is a different way of thinking about organizational life and what it is that managers may intentionally and unintentionally do. Reflexive managers question various interpretations of organizational life and the part they themselves play in creating narrow, exclusionary and potentially manic cultures. This provides a basis for exploring possible re-interpretations of more ethical and responsive ways of managing.

The rest of the chapter focuses on different aspects of culture that managers often take for granted or do not notice. It is organized around three 'critical' themes: obversion, subversion and diversion.

> Obversion – culture as simultaneously managing and manipulating people
>
> Subversion – culture as both conforming and resisting
>
> Diversion – culture as difference

I use these terms with a sense of irony, because they could be seen as catchy buzzwords (well ... maybe only to a few academics!), but also as a way of taking a critical perspective on a number of management issues – a critically-reflexive interrogation of managing culture and an exploration of different ways of thinking about managing organizations.

## Obversion

> Rather than seeking definitions and moving to categorize, we should ask: what are we able to see or think about if we talk about it in this way rather than that? (Alvesson and Deetz, 2000: 43)

Why obversion? The obverse is an opposite or a counterpart to something – but is both opposite and complementary, like two sides of a coin. This draws together two strands we discussed in Chapters 3. First, Derrida's notions of *différance* and *deconstruction*, the idea that words derive meaning from their opposite term, and as those oppositions always interweave it's important to consider alternative readings. Second, the idea that relational, ethical and reflexive managers need to question and examine taken-for-granted ways of thinking and enacting their organization's culture because culture may be simultaneously about:

> What is said and not said
>
> Similarities and differences
>
> Power and empowerment
>
> Conformity and resistance

We'll look at examples of the dialectical relationship between the 'two sides of the coin' throughout the chapter as we explore three major issues of relevance to managing organizations today:

1. Managing culture
2. Power and authority
3. Culture as *man*-aging difference, or the gendered nature of organizations and managing.

It's important for managers to think about these issues through a reflexive lens because they are characteristic of the different ways in which people experience culture, power and identity.

### 'Critical' issues in managing culture

In Chapter 2, we unsettled a few basic assumptions about language, communication and management, and looked at some different ideas based on the view that language *constructs* our world and that our everyday ways of talking are crucial. Within Organization Studies, managing culture is one of the few fields where academics and managers alike recognize the importance of language – but in different ways. Managers and organizational consultants spend a lot of time and energy coming up with compelling (that is, appropriately worded to generate commitment) vision, mission and value statements as a means of creating a culture of ... empowerment, innovation, excellent customer service, _____ ... fill in the gap. Academics take a whole range of epistemological perspectives to study the relationship between language and organizational culture; realists examine how a real existing culture is expressed (represented) through stories, slogans, speeches, jargon and symbols, etc.; social constructionists explore how language shapes 'culture' and identities; poststructuralists deconstruct culture to expose its empty, fragmented and contested nature – the struggles over meaning. Let's take a critically-reflexive look at two different ways of viewing the management of organizational culture: managing culture as D/discourse and managing culture as hyperreal. As we are doing so, ask what is being taken for granted and whether they are examples of managers managing or manipulating culture.

### Managing culture as discourse/discourse

In Chapter 3 we looked at managers as actors and managers of meaning. These ways of thinking connect strongly with managing organizational culture as D/discourse because they are about constructing and maintaining culture through performance and language. The study of culture as D/discourse emerged from the social constructionist emphasis on the constitutive nature of language: that organizational culture is created through naturally occurring talk (conversations – primary speech genres), written text (e.g., emails, documents, statements on company websites), semiotics (physical artifacts and visual images), ways of looking at and talking about the world (Discourse with a capital 'D' – secondary speech genres), and also social action. In other words, from a discursive perspective, language and symbols are important in that they convey meaning (realism) but can also construct social action and be interpreted in multiple ways (social constructionism).

Let's begin with symbols. *Semiotics* is the study of the relationship between meanings and signs, both texts and symbols. A symbol is a signifier because it works as a visual representation conveying meaning – an object, a sound, a form of dress, gesture and emotion. Think of the five interlocking rings of the Olympics representing the union of five continents as an example. Interestingly, Baudrillard (1994) suggests that we consume signs and images that are important for the image they offer us personally. Semiotics is therefore not just important in creating and representing the image of the organization, but is also part of identity-work. For example I might buy a Mercedes, not for the purpose of transporting me from A to B, but because it creates the image that I'm rich, urbane and distinctive ... (not that I have a Mercedes!). Dress and image can be very much part of an organization's culture – you might be surprised, for example, to go into your bank to find an employee wearing shorts and an old T shirt! Many organizations have dress codes, but some reflexive questions to consider are: To what extent are they based on a cultural or gendered norm? Do they suppress individual identities and difference? Do they legitimate power relationships in the organization?

Managers use both language and symbols as part of the process of managing (manipulating?) culture, meaning and identities, and symbolic meanings can draw on emotions, as the example below from my conversation with a Federal Security Director of a US airport shows:[7]

FSD:    See this lanyard? It says 'Team _____'.

Ann:    Uhuh.

FSD:    If you go out, the screeners all have 'Team ____' on the back of their shirts. I want to say, 'Hey – we're in this together', and what happened in New York on September 11th – we can never ever let that happen again. And we can *only* do it if we work together. You know, the adage about a chain being only as strong as its weakest link ...

The lanyard and words 'Team ___' on the shirts indicate cohesion and an identity as a team player. But as we saw in Chapter 2, meaning is context-dependent and variable, so the interpretations of these symbols may vary across employees, passengers and other airport staff. This varying and contested interpretation of words and symbols raises two important critical issues in managing culture, that culture as D/discourse can be problematic if:

1. It is monologic – viewed as fixed, unitary and as a technique of persuasion and manipulation.
2. Organizational D/discourse privileges particular meanings and identities over others.

While we tend to think of language and text as something pretty much fixed, linguist Norman Fairclough (2003) suggests we create meaning through *texturing*, a process of drawing on different texts and semiotic elements in our conversations; combining global and broader social Discourses with local discourses and ways of talking to create and enact new discourses. For example, a couple of years ago a Native American business leader told me that the employees and managers in his organization together created a vision statement that combined two Native American tribal symbols. As an oral society, the broader management Discourse of a written vision statement did not make sense, so they combined it with local ways of talking and living to enact a new discourse – a symbolic vision statement. This example illustrates the dialogic process of texturing where, as Fairclough says, meaning gets concurrently multiplied and sharpened, and takes into consideration local and unique circumstances to identify new alternatives. It's also an illustration of relational and dialogic ways of working because the organization as a community created the vision. From a culture as community of differences perspective, it doesn't make sense to talk about organizations and organizational culture as static entities or objects, but as continual processes of organizing in which organizational members create some sort of shared meaning, in conversation, about what needs to be done.

Language, symbols and stories are very much part of culture as D/discourse: epic stories of organizational heroes, success and victory (see Gabriel and Connell (2010) for examples of critical experiments in storytelling). It's interesting to note that language and storytelling have become commodified – a Marxist idea in which something is given economic value in the market. In this case, whereas storytelling is a natural part of everyday interaction, it has now become a product to be sold and to be consumed by others – a tool for change. A UK consulting company, The Storytellers, helps companies use stories to 'drive strategic engagement and behavioural change'.[8] Managers are trained in the four basic components and techniques of good business storytelling. A recent book, *Storytelling in Organizations* (Prusak et al., 2011), talks about how managers can use narratives and stories as tools for change. Stories are persuasive and powerful because people can connect with the plot (strategic vision and goals), can visualize situations more easily and know what character they have to play.

While using stories, symbols and rhetoric to create meaning and connection with an organization's culture and history may seem benign, a reflexive manager asks to what degree are D/discourse and stories monologic and manipulative? Does storying culture in this way privilege a particular view, ideology or identity? On page 82, I mentioned the influence of Peters and Waterman's book *In Search of Excellence*: their approach is based on 'epic' stories of successful companies and presents a monologic Discourse of eight 'excellent' characteristics to be reproduced by other companies. David Collins argues that in Peters' pre-1996 work, women are rarely key characters but have supporting 'walk-on parts in a larger pageant' (2012: 414). Around 1996, Peters began to recognize that business didn't appreciate women and advised female employees to 'roar' their discontent. His post-1996 discourse is of advising (often male) managers to 'take advantage' of the skills of women employees (Collins, 2012: 421). Why does this continue to privilege a monologic culture? Having seen Tom Peters present, 'roaring' appears to be his style – a style admired and probably emulated by those audience members who want to become 'excellent' managers … regardless of gender, race or ethnic differences. What identity-struggles may arise as a result? And does the language 'taking advantage of' give you the sense that there is a genuine intention to make a difference to the opportunities for women in the workplace? You might want to complete Tom's leadership self-assessment on his website, with a reflexive eye on the language.[9]

So if we understand organizational culture from a reflexive, relational and ethical perspective, as an interweaving of Discourses and discourse, what does this mean? That managers need to think about organizational culture as:

- Emerging *all the time* in our actions, conversations, texts and symbols, whether we are aware of it or not.
- Open to many interpretations and reinterpretations – to *texturing* – in lived experience.
- Privileging particular ideologies and groups, a form of manipulation, whether intentional or otherwise.

## Managing the hyperreal: culture as simulacra

In Chapter 3 we looked at performativity, the idea that we talk and act things into reality. French social philosopher Jean Baudrillard takes performativity further, arguing that it is no longer possible to talk about what is real because the image becomes the reality. In his 1994 book, *Simulacra and Simulations*, he claimed that the distinction between the real and the sign or image has broken down, and that there isn't a real original any more – just an image that masks the absence of reality. Imagine working in an organization where you have an annual obligatory 'employee retreat' to revisit the mission, vision and values statements in an open, transparent and collaborative forum. Most employees view this activity with cynicism because they experience a culture of bullying, favouritism and intimidation – yet they go along with the image and talk-the-talk to maintain the pretence or simulation. Simulacra can be nostalgic – trying to reproduce a lost reality, such as the reproduction of an organizational culture of traditional family values when the original family who started and built the organization is no longer involved. Simulacra can also be a simulation of an ideal or the not-yet-real, a company, the media or a government presenting information and images to create an event or situation that doesn't exist. Baudrillard calls this *hyperreality*, an interactive performance or simulation in which we are trying to produce what we think is real, but which is only an image.

Imagine working in a large glass-clad structure built to eliminate boundaries and bring you closer to the customer and community by blending the inside and outside; an open-plan design with no interior walls and with modern chrome and glass furniture. You are expected to dress in casual clothes, talk and act in particular ways, to have the 'WOW!' factor: to be creative, fun, happy, helpful and do what it takes to put internal and external customers first. This is hyperreality, and is different from Goffman's performance in at least one essential way: for Baudrillard the simulation becomes the real, the distinction breaks down between the sign and the signified, the fake and the authentic. There are also tensions of identity in a simulacra: you are expected to 'be your real fun self' all day (is this possible?!), to be who you are – yet conform to expectations. You walk through the door and either instinctively become the WOW! person: the successful manipulation of culture, of identity and of hearts, minds and souls. It is also an illustration of what critical scholars call the *colonization of the self* in that it's a culture that controls who you are, how you think and act, and how you relate to others. While simulating freedom, it uses normative forms of control that appeal to the values and feelings of people. For example, is asking employees to sing a 'meaningful family' song together at the beginning of each day a form of self-expression and fun, or of control? In their study of call centres, Fleming and Sturdy (2011) argue that this type of culture is not about freedom *from* control, but freedom *around* control. Which brings us to the issue of power ...

## Culture and power: 'I got the power'... and the authority and the responsibility

> And when they go to their bosses, they say, 'I don't want to know about layouts! I don't want to resolve the issues with the lawyers', who all work for Corporate. Literally, none of the lawyers can make a decision for the rest of the group, and there are 8 lawyers. We have to talk to every single one to get agreement. And there's no leverage! And I think there are a lot of groups around here where it's a similar kind of thing. Information Technology has a steering committee that is trying to look out into the future. To what degree do people say, 'Yes, I agree to give my authority to the steering committee and abide by its decisions'? (Programme manager talking about authority issues in a project)

Organizations run on authority structures and organizational culture defines through mission and values statements how power is operationalized and how employees act towards each other and their managers. One of the first things you learn in Management 101, is the relationship between authority, responsibility and accountability. Scholars in the era of the systematization of management were concerned with clarifying and establishing managerial authority and differentiating managers from others through the nature of their responsibilities. Authority is typically seen as the right to give orders and to enforce rules – it's about legitimate power – monologic ways of speaking. Responsibility is the obligation to achieve goals, make specified decisions and perform certain tasks, for which you are held accountable, that is, answerable to your boss. The key is ensuring that a manager's authority is commensurate with responsibility, so that she or he has the power to get things done. Organizational culture is about defining and representing the nature of the authority relationship, for example as centralized, autonomous, individual or team-based.

However, as you can see in the above quote from a programme manager, power is complex: it not only involves authority and responsibility, it also requires establishing relationships, getting commitment and persuading others over whom you have no authority. And, as you might now imagine, there are different views on what power is, how it plays out in practice and who should have it. From a rational and realist perspective, power is vested in a hierarchical position, is a manager's prerogative and managerial authority is unquestionably legitimate. These are often known as bureaucratic cultures. Critical scholars challenge the distribution of power throughout society and the right of particular groups (owners, shareholders, managers) to dominate and control others. From a social constructionist perspective, power is embedded within social practices and relationships. Other than giving a brief overview, I don't want to spend too much time talking about rational and realist constructions of power, authority and responsibility, because you can read about these in any management book. I do want to explore some alternative ways of thinking about these issues that offer possibilities for managing and thinking differently about organizational relationships.

## The power and the glory ...

In mainstream management and organization theory, managers (as rational agents) are apportioned the right to have authority over others, with a corresponding responsibility for outcomes. Power is some*thing* associated with a particular position and level in an organization, and authority often draws on Max Weber's idea of rational-legal authority. This takes us back to the idea that management is about representing and intervening – a culture based on clear rules, procedures, jobs, tasks, goals, and intervening through the division of labour, de-skilling work and setting up measurement systems to control employee performance. Power and authority are also represented discursively and semiotically in *talk*, *signs*, *texts* and *symbols*: a manager giving instructions to an employee, a job title, a job description, a large office, a company car and a parking space. Much of the literature in the field is concerned with how managers can influence others and gain power by creating situations where other organizational members are dependent upon them because they have the knowledge, expertise, resources and/or information that others need, or because they can resolve critical organizational problems (e.g., Kotter, 1977; Pfeffer, 1992; Salancik and Pfeffer, 1977).

From a conventional managerialist perspective, authority is transcendent, legitimate and monologic. By this, I mean that authority is vested in a position regardless of the person holding it; it legitimates the manager's right to control the actions and behaviours of others; and monologic because it establishes who has the right to speak and who doesn't. Bakhtin (1986: 163) suggests the process of monologization occurs when dialogic voices are assimilated into one voice, in this case the managerial voice of authority. And danger lies in managers having too much power. In *The Hubris Syndrome* (2012) David Owen examines how political leaders such as George W. Bush and Tony Blair became intoxicated by power and exhibited hubristic behaviour. Such behaviour includes: a narcissistic view of the world as a place to exercise power, being overly concerned with self-image, overconfidence and an inflated self-belief. Not only does this sound like Stein's (2011) manic culture, it exemplifies a relationship in which self rather than others is the focus of attention!

From a critical perspective, rational approaches to authority are processes of distinction and consent, and an effect of historical, economic, political, social and therefore ideological forces. When someone becomes a manager, she or he becomes a member of, and identifies with, a group, a profession or a class that is distinct from other groups – a distinction shaped by history, discourse and social practices, and maintained by those in authority and those under authority. Bakhtin talks about how *authoritative discourse* (for example, scientific truth or managerialism) gets its power:

> The authoritative word demands that we acknowledge it, that we make it our own; it binds us, quite independent of any power it might have to persuade us internally; we encounter it with its authority already fused to it. The authoritative word is located in a distanced zone, organically connected with a past that is felt to be hierarchically higher. It is, so to speak, the word of the fathers ... It is therefore not a question of choosing it from among other possible discourses that are its equal. (1981: 342)

In other words, we accept the authority of management discourse and the Discourse of management authority, and let them define our ideological relationship with the world: not necessarily because we are persuaded by their legitimacy, but because we take their form of reasoning as a given truth and they seem a natural part of organizational life – an accepted culture. Such discourses, Bakhtin says, enter our consciousness as static, complete and inflexible – demanding our unconditional allegiance. For example, we might complain about organizational cultures and Discourses that are overly bureaucratic and controlling, but we accept them as a given.

It was not until the advent of CMS that alternative discourses and new voices emerged that engaged in questioning the nature of 'modern' management and organizations. Which brings us to the idea that critical scholars take a transgressive view of managerial power, arguing that we need to look at alternative readings, at the relationship between control and resistance, domination and submission, and to uncover the insidious nature of power relationships. But why should we do so? Because a critically-reflexive examination of authority structures, and their intended and unintended consequences, can form the basis for discovering more human and ethical ways of managing.

Critical scholars analyse the structural mechanisms, the ideologies and the communication processes that lead to cultures in which employees are exploited. They do so with the aim of creating more democratic forms of governance and working. As we saw in Chapter 1, critics of ideology question the assumption that capitalist and managerialist ideologies legitimate owners' and managers' rights to dominate workers. They also explore how this domination occurs in ways of which we may be unaware. Karl Marx argued that workers participate in their own exploitation by accepting an owner's or a manager's right to give orders. Italian Marxist theorist Antonio Gramsci (1971) used the concept of *hegemony* to explain why this happens, why dominated groups are not necessarily coerced into conforming, but spontaneously and actively consent to being dominated. He claims this is because institutional and ideological values, and the structures, systems and practices that support them, become part of our everyday taken-for-granted activities, and so influence us throughout our life in subtle and incessant ways – they become 'normal' to us.

This might explain why we participate in hyperreal cultures and in the colonization of the self that we discussed earlier. However ... in succumbing to hegemonic practices they work against our interests by restricting our personal choices. For example, what if you are given greater autonomy in your job? You have more discretion over your work, can do what you want, when you want, and you can manage yourself ... a good thing you might think ... You decide to take on a challenging project, which means working 15 hours a day and a few weekends to finish it. You do so quite happily because you have 'autonomy'. Would you have worked 80 hours a week without extra pay and spent little time with family and friends if your manager had asked you to do so? Steven Lukes (1974) calls this insidious form of power the *third face of power* – it doesn't take into consideration differences: divergent values, interests or practices, or alternative ways of organizing work. Ironically his way of working is typical of 'strong' cultures (Deal and Kennedy, 1982) that emphasize autonomy and commitment.

Hegemony involves a constant struggle, not just over power, but also over identity. Consider these comments made by an MBA student:

> I had something to prove. Being only 27 ... no military background, did not graduate from an Ivy League or equivalent, and worked for a family business ... In addition, I carried the baggage of racial and economic discrimination from both my parents' and personal experiences.

I realize now that I suffered from a poor self-image. I had an inferiority complex that fueled my passion and work ethic. I needed to prove that I was better than my white, Ivy League, affluent, experienced peers. If they were smarter, then I would work harder. But I would be damned to concede that they were any better.

You may feel the student's frustration as he feels difference – comparing himself to others (ethnically, educationally, his work identity) and attempting to resolve struggle with those differences by working harder. His comments also illustrate that hegemony is not an abstract concept, but a lived experience that involves the control of emotions, hearts and minds; how hegemony is an attempt to ignore distinctions in order to maintain power and a social/identity norm; and how in this case resistance is ironically a form of compliance that benefits the very group the student was resisting and to which he felt he had something to prove – something he discovered later when he found his manager taking the recognition for his work. His comments also illustrate the frustration that can occur when managers remain insensitive to difference.

### Culture as man-aging difference

> Yet our direct experience tells us that organizational cultures – as holistic phenomena – are strongly 'gendered'. Organizations themselves, therefore, are gendered, and organizational processes are ways of organizing gender relations. (Gherardi, 1995: 12)

I've mentioned before the gendered nature of management and organizations, and that the dark side of culture is about minimizing differences such as gender and ethnicity, But what does this mean? Because this is a *Very Short…* book, I'm going to address gender particularly and briefly look at other differences; however, the issues relate to all differences.

Often the first thought on gender is that it's about the position and pay of women in organizations. Recent surveys show that gender inequality still exists. Shin's (2012) study of directors and CEOs in the USA found that of 7,711 executives, 6 per cent were women, who on average were paid $440,000 less than men. The UK's *Sex and Power 2013* report (Centre for Women and Democracy, 2013) found that women make up only 10.9 per cent of FTSE250 directors, 22.5 per cent of MPs. The UK Office of National Statistics (2012) found that British women in general earn £100 less per week than men. In Australia (2012), only 9.2 per cent of executives in the ASX500 are women, and on average women earn 18 per cent less than men.[10] The number of sexual discrimination lawsuits filed in the US has increased over last 10 years. In 2013, the highest-ranking nurse in the British Royal Air Force won a sex discrimination case against the Ministry of Defence after a male with less experience was promoted to a position both applied for. To put it bluntly, as Sheryl Sandberg, chief operating officer of Facebook, says in her book *Lean In: Women, Work and the Will to Lead*, 'men still run the world' (2013: 5).

Yet statistics are only part of the story – numbers objectify the embodied lived experience of gendered work and organizations.

Gendered organizations are not just about statistics and whether the organization has day-care facilities, but also about who is in power, who does what type of work, what normative expectations influence behaviour and attitudes, what type of language is spoken, and how organizational members are evaluated, rewarded and promoted. Organizations are gendered linguistically, semiotically and practically, in taken-for-granted ways of acting and being. Practically, particular types of work are typically seen as women's work (the caring professions: secretarial, nursing, teaching), and women play supportive roles as secretaries and assistants to a patriarchal social order of male dominance. Women as well as men often take for granted what is accepted as 'the norm' and what is enacted as being different. As critical communication theorists Karen Ashcraft and Dennis Mumby say: 'Put simply, women appear as visibly gendered "others", while men are erased as the genderless norm' (2004: xiv). In other words, the 'white maleness' of organizations remains unquestioned, while non-white, non-maleness is emphasized through activities such as the setting up of women and minority advisory committees and mentor networks. In effect, such committees and networks reinforce power inequalities and boundaries because they are outside the 'normal' structure and practice, and serve to differentiate and exclude groups rather than include them.

This process of differentiation was really brought home in the way the media (both men and women) treated Hillary Clinton during her run for the Presidential candidacy. Watch the video montage of the media treatment of Hillary Clinton,[11] which includes comments such as: 'Her hair looked great', 'If she knew how it made her look …', 'Men won't vote for Hillary Clinton because she reminds them of their nagging wives', 'The reason she's a US senator, the reason she's a candidate for President … is her husband messed around … She didn't win on her merit', and so on. Were the same comments being made about her male counterparts?! This seemingly egregious – yet frighteningly real – example highlights women as 'visibly gendered others'.

We encountered the gendered, ethnocentric and performative nature of management Discourse in Chapter 1 – how the ever-present discourse of rationality requires masculine skills and forms of behaviour (control, authority, discipline, objectivity, individuality, competitiveness, assertiveness, and so on) that non-male, non-white employees are often expected to emulate. The role of Discourse (language systems) and discourse (everyday ways of talking) in reinforcing gendered norms can be seen in the way pregnancy was treated in the US. From the 1960s onwards, pregnancy was classed legally as a *temporary disability* in which pregnant women could not be treated any more or less favourably than employees with other disabilities. Business associations argued that health insurance and disability plans should not be extended to cover pregnancy and childbirth, because childbirth was a voluntary condition! In addition, the definition of a disability as a physical or mental impairment that substantially limits carrying out normal life activities frames childbirth as a non-normal event that lessens a woman's ability to carry out her work in quality ways and continue to be committed to the organization. It wasn't until the 1993 Family and Medical Leave Act that both male and female employees had the right to take unpaid leave to care for the birth, adoption or foster care of her or his child.

Organization sociologist Silvia Gherardi (1995) suggests that the presence of women, especially in male-gendered cultures, involves both men and women in the 'remedial work' of restoring gendered order. She uses a storied or narrative approach to talk about how women deal with D/discourses of femaleness within organizational D/discourses of maleness that can be friendly or hostile:

**Table 4.1**   Discursive positions of women in a male culture

| | |
|---|---|
| Friendly cultures | *Women as guests:* treated politely, being protected and looked after, yet given women's tasks (talking to people on the phone) and always in a subordinated position. |
| | *Women as holidaymakers:* seen as just passing through, conforming to past practices, not feeling 'at home' and thus not able to change things. |
| | *Women as newcomers:* seen as a curiosity, but not as 'a real man'. Judged on her ability to integrate. |
| Hostile cultures | *Women as marginal:* tolerated yet invisible, expected to obey, agree and wait for decisions, not allowed to question or contribute to discussions. |
| | *Women as the snake in the grass:* seen as the enemy who confronts and changes the 'normal' rather than conforming. |
| | *Women as intruders:* who position themselves as equal yet who are actively resisted by others. |

Source: based on Gherardi (1995: 108–22)

These are discursive and relational positions in that they are enacted, resisted, negotiated and perhaps changed in the everyday interactions of both male and female organizational members. The discursive construction of gender in male-gendered cultures is also evident in politics. For example, former UK Prime Minister Margaret Thatcher was labelled 'The Iron Lady' because she was 'strong willed' (does this mean determined and decisive, or headstrong and wilful?!). You might want to look at former Australian Prime Minister Julia Gillard's 2012 response to Leader of the Opposition Tony Abbott's comment regarding sexism.[12]

The lived experience of gender at work is also about language. Not only in terms of how gender plays out practically in different conversational styles that result in whose comments are more likely to be recognized, remembered and rewarded (see Tannen's 1995 and 2001 work for examples), but also through linguistic oppositions. We talk about 'hard' technical skills versus 'soft' people skills, public versus private, rational versus emotional, and so on – oppositions associated with being masculine or feminine, in which one is privileged over the other. This oppositional way of seeing situations, and the tensions this can raise for women managers, can be seen in the comment by a female manager during our discussion about her work:

> I was talking to someone today who said they'd heard that I was one of those women who's tough for the sake of being tough, but that actually they thought I was very nice! And I said, 'Oh? Okay!' I had two reactions to it; one is that it means you are the virgin or the whore – as a woman you either get to be tough or nice but somehow you can't be both …

Others share her experience of the tensions of gendered identity, especially in predominantly masculine professions and cultures. In her study of women in UK and US accounting and law firms, Kathryn Haynes (2012) found there were acceptable *bodily norms* and *embodied identities* at work that affected hiring, promotion, rewards and relationships with clients. Such bodily norms relate to gender, race, class, age, disability and sexuality, and also to issues such as dress (e.g., wearing tailored suits) and demeanour (speech and manner). For example, in relation to the latter, women found themselves having to balance gendered expectations in terms of being a powerful advocate (male) or perceived as 'too shrill' (female). Some firms wanted staff to appear fit and healthy, which resulted in women being conscious about fitting the bodily norm, and being seen as too young, overweight or too short impacted credibility and resulted in marginalization or managing one's body, e.g., by being the best dressed. In other words, women managers and employees have to deal with the tensions of masculinity and femininity so that they can actively participate in predominantly masculine cultures (Brewis, 1999).

The experience of identity-work is therefore also about body-work. And from the perspective of managers as discursive subjectivities, the body is not only visibly gendered, but also a site of subordination to organizational ideals, and when female managers draw upon masculine signifiers as a way of participating, this reinforces the gendered discourse of management, identity and organizations (Pullen, 2006).

Differences of gender are not the only concern of Critical Management Studies. A number of critical scholars study the racialized nature of organizations. Bobby Banerjee and Deirdre Tedmanson (2010) examine how indigenous entrepreneurs in Australia are subject to the ideological discourse of 'whiteness'. Terms such as 'non-whites' are ideological in the sense that being 'white' is privileged and being 'non-white' implies you are lacking. For example, clients of an Aboriginal owner of a tourism business often asked to see his boss and indigenous community representative councils are expected to operate using western bureaucratic forms of administration rather than traditional forms of collective governance. Discourses of whiteness are dominant because they are the taken-for-granted norm against which expectations and judgements are made – judgements that marginalize and ignore different ways of being a manager or entrepreneur and different cultural and organizing practices.

Stephen Fineman's (2011) book, *Organizing Age*, addresses another form of difference, looking at how age is socially constructed and performative (remember Judith Butler's work on gender in Chapter 3), and how this plays out in organizational culture. For example, young people have to 'prove their worth', while older people are 'past it' (whatever 'it' is). These differences are very much tied up with identity-work as people are classed as being different – a 'minority' employee, an 'older worker' – and try to cope with the often resulting stigmatization. The controversy continues regarding ageism and sexism in the media industry as 'older' female TV presenters are forcibly retired while their male counterparts continue to work.

We've just touched the surface of how difference is embedded within organizational culture, and yet organizational culture can be experienced as monologic – silencing some voices and privileging others. Organizational culture is also performative: in the sense that differences are created and maintained in organizational Discourse and in everyday interactions, a process of social construction in which both men and women produce and reproduce gender distinctions in conscious or unconscious ways by uncritically enacting and accepting those differences (hegemony).

While management theory and practice do address difference through diversity management and equal opportunity – we need to reflexively ask, 'What is being taken for granted?' How are privileges of gender, race, age, sexual orientation, etc., created and maintained in everyday practices? How are differences 'managed'? In the latter, the strategy is often related to using the skills and knowledge of those who are different from us (inferior in some way?) to improve the competitiveness of the organization. What are the implications of such a strategy for the responsive and ethical management of differences?

### Subversion: resistance is futile … or is it?

Lisa:   My predecessor had a picture on the wall – it was a team thing – one of those hunting metaphors with male hunters chasing men in deerskins (our competitors) – but it was so male and they didn't get it.

Ann:    The images of aggression and masculinity?

Lisa:   Yes, and in meetings they use baseball and football metaphors – so I thought I'm not using any sporting metaphors, I'm creating my own.

Subversion implies the undermining or overthrowing of something – at a minimum it implies non-compliance and, beyond this, rebellion or revolution. Critical Management Studies is not just about obversion – understanding the taken-for-granted power structures and hegemonic practices that lead to intended and unintended injustices of modern management – but also about finding ways of destabilizing, subverting and changing those injustices. Of course, not every manager in every organization is deliberately engaging in oppressive actions, but managing critically means being reflexive about how we may unintentionally marginalize others through our assumptions, relationships and interactions: about knowing what is and what is not ethical. The quote above, an excerpt from my research conversation with Lisa, a project manager in a large high-tech organization, highlights the power relationships and gender differences embedded within everyday symbols and conversations that are a taken-for-granted part of organizational life. Her response – creating her own metaphors – was a linguistic act of resistance.

Lisa's final comment is also an example of what Critical Communication scholar Dennis Mumby (2005) sees as the dialectical process of control and resistance – that resistance is not just a form of subversion, but is simultaneously about control *and* resistance, about enabling action *and* constraining it, about drawing on D/discourses that are coherent *and* contradictory, which can create tensions in identity-work. In Lisa's case, she was both resisting and attempting to deal with and control by using her own metaphors. We will see more examples of this dialectical process below.

Theorizing and studying various forms of resistance are a central concern within critical approaches. Alessia Contu (2008), for example, differentiates between 'real' acts of resistance that change the order of things and have a cost (e.g., whistleblowing, taking a grievance against a bullying manager) and more subtle 'decaf' acts of resistance in which, like decaf coffee, we can engage but they carry no cost (e.g., withdrawing effort or engaging in theft, dishonesty or sabotage). For example, Prasad and Prasad (2001) found routine and subtle acts of resistance to the computerization of work in a health care organization. Employees engaged in mundane acts of resistance such as 'careful carelessness' (spilling coffee on keyboards, forgetting to save data, accidentally misfiling information), sabotage and 'dumb resistance' (such as a reluctance to use personal judgement). For employees, the artful subversion of managerial authority took on heroic proportions and managers found it difficult to deal with actions that could be perceived as being unintentional.

We'll now look at ways in which both managers and employees resist what they feel are threats to their identity and sense of self, through a 'critical' social constructionist perspective, which sees resistance as constructed within the talk and the interactions of organizational participants – participants who themselves will have differing interpretations of what is 'real' and to be resisted.

### Discursive resistance

The comments made by Lisa (above) about sports metaphors and cartoons illustrate the discursive and symbolic aspects of hegemony. Ernest Laclau and Chantal Mouffe (1985) suggest that discursive hegemony occurs when one discourse prevails and becomes the dominant interpretive framework through which conversations, actions and identities pass and become redefined. A current example in UK academic life is prevailing discourse of the 2014 Research Excellence Framework (REF), in which the identity of individual academics centres around the discourse of whether one is 'REF-able' (worthy to be submitted in the university's REF document) and is a '4 x 4' (has four 4-star publications).

However, hegemony is also spatial and symbolic in the sense that space and place are saturated with semiotic meanings. Typical cultural artifacts such as company cars, a large corner office, type and size of desk and chair, maintain distinctions of power and identity. Such meanings are based on the background conversations of organizational members, conversations that have 'a particular coherence [...] such that within that reality, everything is appropriate' (Ford, Ford and McNamara, 2002: 109). And because this coherence is taken for granted, alternative views and resistance to the 'norm' are difficult.

While we typically think of resistance in terms of non-managerial employees, managers also find themselves resisting organizational culture. Robyn Thomas and Annette Davis (2005) argue that resistance and identity-work are interwoven, both taking place as 'individuals confront, and reflect on, their own identity performance, recognizing contradictions and tensions and, in so doing, pervert and subtly shift meanings and understandings' (2005: 687). In their study of how managers attempt to deal, discursively, with feelings of difference, and to resist the normalizing discourse of the New Public Management (NPM) culture, they found individual managers attempting to deal with the tensions of three main discursive NPM managerial subjectivities:

- a competitive, pushy, target-oriented masculine subjectivity
- a disempowered, loyal, unquestioning subjectivity
- a feminized, tolerant, respectful subjectivity.

For example, one police inspector constructed himself as a 'maverick' (too outspoken and friendly) rather than a 'clone' who conforms without question – a form of resistance against disempowered subjectivity. Their study is also an example of the dialectics of control and resistance in that it explores how managers deal with the tensions and contradictions in what could easily be assumed to be a coherent NPM discourse. See also Jackie Ford's (2006) study of how public sector managers dealt with discursive ambiguity by adopting a range of subject positions.

Relational, reflexive and ethical managers need to be sensitive to the discursive and interpretive struggles within background conversations, to the ways in which different groups and individuals talk about situations and experiences, to hegemonic organization stories and stories of resistance (e.g., Boje, 2008; Brown and Humphreys, 2006), how these ways of talking might be tied to identity, and how different meanings may be recognized and accepted.

### Resisting through humour

Managing hearts, minds and bodies has emotional consequences for those being managed, as we saw in Chapter 3. And one way of dealing with the emotional consequences of culture and identity-work is through humour. Resistance through humour can be seen as the part of organizational life that Yiannis Gabriel (1995) suggests is, and should be, unmanageable. The unmanaged organization reflects a spontaneous, emotional, *fantasy* life of stories, gossip and jokes: fantasy in that stories of real events are embellished and imbued with different meanings and significance. I'm reminded of an event that occurred years ago at my place of work. A senior manager got her hand stuck in the coffee vending machine, reaching up to pull down a miscreant cup. The Fire Service arrived to cut her hand out, closely followed by an ambulance and a police car. The manager was rather an autocratic and exacting person, the bane of trainees' lives because they felt she monitored their every move. The irony of the situation was not lost upon them, and the story took on epic proportions, including a (fantasy) ending with the manager being carried out of the building by a burly fireman! Trainees were careful to ensure they had a cup of vending machine coffee when attending meetings with her.

This unmanaged space incorporated both humorous stories and symbolic forms of resistance, which Gabriel suggests is often a response to being over-managed and over-controlled. Humour was – and is – important because it helped trainees cope with what were often demanding and stressful interactions; gave them a 'voice' (although indirectly) where they normally had to be silent, and also a sense of camaraderie. Humour can also be about creating a 'better' alternative reality. In a study of 'monotonous' and 'brain dead' factory work, Marek Korczynski (2011: 1431) found that workers used routine humour, absurdity, clowning around and music to mock management and the work process and to construct a 'stayin' alive' culture of their own, which made work more tolerable.

### Is resistance futile?

We've looked at various forms of resisting monologic cultures, and in the example above, workers created their own counter-culture to help them deal with the frustrations of boring work. But these forms of resistance didn't change the 'formal' culture. Employees sometimes find themselves facing situations where they believe resistance *is* futile.

One such example is Joyce Fletcher's (1998) study of female engineers, whom she found managed their own difference. Many tried to engage in *relational practices*, feminine beliefs valuing mutual empathy and empowerment, which included preserving the well-being of a project, enabling oneself and others to contribute to projects and working collaboratively in teams. However, the dominant organizational culture valued individual competitiveness, recognized and rewarded autonomy, self-promotion and individual heroics. Relational practices were ignored, seen as 'mothering', or exploited by the male engineers. Rather than resist the prevailing D/discourse, the female engineers, while wanting to work differently, *disappeared* their own relational practices, by talking about relational behaviours as weak and inappropriate for work and warning female colleagues of the consequences of engaging in such behaviours.

The implications of Fletcher's work for relational and reflexive managing are threefold. Managers need to change:

1. managerial practices that continue to reinforce gendered definitions of competence and success that exclude other equally valid ways of contributing
2. a culture where employees feel pressured into suppressing their own differences and equally valid ways of working and interacting
3. a culture where any form of questioning the 'norm' is met by reprisals.

An example of where resistance was not futile can be seen in Hester Eisenstein's (1996) study of women in government positions in Australia. A group of senior women (named femocrats) engaged in enacting policies that advanced women's interests in a bureaucracy and a policy environment that reflected men's interests. It's a fascinating study of how a group of women with an agenda of social change managed to deal with the contradictions and tensions of conflicting identities: of remaining both active feminists and 'good bureaucrats'. Although criticized by the political right for being too radical, and by the women's movement for not being radical enough, this group of influential women challenged the male power structure in state bureaucracy. They set up a central women's affairs office for policy purposes, had a clear agenda for change and won funding for women's initiatives. A strategy of resistance through coordinated action.

The point I hope I'm making is that if we consider culture as obversive, an ongoing tension between managers and employees, organization and disorganization, managed and unmanaged, power and resistance, feminine and masculine, and so on, then issues of culture, power, identity, gender and language become interrelated and multifaceted aspects of managing organizations. Consequently, relational and reflexive managers need to be aware of the invisible and moral, as well as the visible and seemingly benign, aspects of culture: to be sensitive to the tensions and relationship with the 'other', to what is said and unsaid, and to be open to the possibilities for change that difference offers. Relational and reflexive managers also look for differences between their espoused theories and theories-in-action, between what they say and what they do (see Argyris, 1991).


## Diversion

> *I don't know*
> *if humankind understands*
> *culture: the act*
> *of being human*
> *is not easy knowledge. (Ortiz, 2002)*

Issues of diversity are very personal and unless you confront them in a personal way, organizations just aren't going to get anywhere. It's about how do I get L___ to fit into this white, male-oriented organization – because there *is* going to come a point at which I say: No! I'm not going to give up who I am to do that. The question to me is to what degree does the organization want me or other kinds of people, and be willing to accept there are other ways of behaving and acting and to become more cognizant that there are norms that are culturally based and gender based, and the advantage of having women in the organization and respecting differences .... Unless the organization is open to that, it is not going to be especially effective. (Lisa, project manager in a large high-tech company)

I hope you now have the sense that managing culture is not as straightforward as some make it out to be, that culture can be a means of control and manipulation, of managing identities, hearts and minds, and privileging some groups over others, as Kunda suggests. Also that culture is not about creating monologic mission, vision and values statements that make everyone the same. The quote above from Simon Ortiz, Native American poet from Acoma, not only brings us back to the story of emergence in the Introduction, but highlights that culture is complex and potentially dehumanizing, and that understanding how to be a decent human being can be difficult – a point reinforced by the project manager's comments that her organization is not open to difference.

So what are the possibilities for change? I'd like to end this chapter by looking at some different considerations in managing organizations. We'll begin by thinking about 'difference' from a relational, reflexive and ethical perspective, and then how relational, reflexive and ethical managers might create organizational cultures as communities of difference.

## Managing difference or making a difference?

Managing difference is not about minimizing difference – a deficit model (Agar, 1994) that is based on how *you* need to adapt and be integrated into *my* way of doing things, because you are going to be evaluated on *my* criteria. Neither is it training people to think and act like the norm through such programmes as 'Dress for Success' or 'Communicating Assertively'. As we have seen, most management techniques, processes and procedures are concerned with reducing people to the same, and events, policies and processes to their simplest common denominator. Maslow's Hierarchy of Needs (1943) is a classic example of a general theory of motivation that makes gendered and ethnic assumptions about how everyone should behave and what their purpose in life should be – to self-actualize. What we've seen is that reducing life to generalizations misses a great deal. Organizations are not simple structures but complex interweavings of people and their emotions, meanings, interpretations, actions, assumptions, bodies, and ways of talking that often favour one group and make others invisible …

## Managing relationally: culture as communities of difference

Linguistic anthropologist Michael Agar has an interesting view of culture. He says that we tend to think of culture as some*thing* that groups of people have: it tells us who we are, our national, organizational or group identity, how the world works, what we value and how we see the rest of the world. But, he says, culture is more than that; it's also about how we relate to others, 'what happens to *you* when you encounter differences, become aware of something in yourself, and work to figure out why the differences appeared. Culture is an awareness, a consciousness, one that reveals the hidden self and opens paths to other ways of being' (1994: 20). Which connects with our theme of relationality, reflexivity and identity-work.

Agar's ideas become relevant to managers when he talks about how we deal with differences within a multicultural world. Some people see difference as a threat and take a deficit approach to dealing with the situation – what does the other culture or person lack when compared to me and my (superior) culture, and how do I remedy that? This involves a monologic process of socialization and colonization: expecting or requiring the 'other' person of a different race, religion, gender or ethnicity to subordinate their values, beliefs and actions to mine. Colonization can occur both on a one-to-one basis between managers and employees and at an organizational level. For example, in some cultures, listening is valued and direct eye contact is a sign of disrespect, so is it colonization if a manager requires an employee from that culture to 'act assertively' if she or he wants to get promoted?

If you've experienced a company merger or acquisition, you may be familiar with this deficit process as one organizational culture subsumes the other. Another example is Viktorija Kalonaityte's (2010) study of diversity management in a Swedish school, where despite the government's focus on social justice and pro-diversity initiatives, immigrant teachers and ethnic minority students were assimilated and integrated into the community based on the binary conceptualization and assumption of a 'superior' modern Swedish democratic culture versus an 'inferior' superstitious and traditional immigrant culture – Agar's deficit approach. Kalonaityte argues that we should question the borders and boundaries that separate insiders from outsiders, and reflexively explore the ambivalent spaces where inconsistencies and resistance can occur. For example, where democracy and autonomy are proclaimed, yet alternative viewpoints are silenced. It is also a form of silencing if a manager says, 'we leave our differences at the door, everyone is treated the same here' ... usually treating people 'the same' means the same as the taken-for-granted cultural norm. The need to explore these ambivalent spaces is clear, even from a purely instrumental perspective! Agar asks, 'In a business negotiation where X knows a great deal about Y, and Y knows almost nothing about X, who has the advantage?' (1994: 24).

What if we view culture as 'an awareness, a consciousness, one that reveals the hidden self and opens paths to other ways of being' (Agar, 1994: 20)? Then managing is not about managing differences from the deficit model, but managing relationally, reflexively and ethically – recognizing that differences are rich opportunities to learn something about ourselves and others, because differences make us aware not only of what we take for granted in our own culture, but also of new ways of seeing, saying and doing, i.e., culture as difference is about identity-work. This also brings us back to Bakhtin's notion of heteroglossia, the importance of recognizing the many languages, speech genres, meanings, ways of talking and of seeing – and of employing speech tact. As he says:

> The better our command of genres, the more freely we employ them, the more fully we reveal our own individuality in them (where this is possible and necessary), the more flexibly and precisely we reflect

the unrepeatable situation of communication – in a word, the more perfectly we implement our free speech plan. (Bakhtin, 1986: 80)

His 'free speech plan' consists of intentions, actions and relationships that are genuine and sincere. This might sound unrealistic, but a group of New Zealand consultants, *Storymaker Partners*, claim to use a relational approach to leadership and change by working with managers on how to engage in dialogue by 'listening closely, and noticing moments when, for instance, other forms of expression would open up new possibilities'.[13] You might see a connection between their approach and Bakhtin's ideas, also the idea that relational managers understand the importance of working with differences and act with integrity and sincerity, and should think reflexively about the nature of language, dialogue and symbols.

Basically, managing organizations as communities of difference means 'being committed to a creative analysis of difference, power and privilege' (Fine, Weis and Powell, 1997: 249).

### Relational responsibility

I've argued that power and control are key elements of culture that need to be reflexively interrogated, that we need to think about culture as communities of difference and that relational managers manage in ethical and responsible ways. We'll look at ethics in the next chapter, but for now let us look at how we might think about power and 'responsibility' differently. In particular, I want to offer a relational and dialogic view of responsibility that takes into account the need to be open to others, to various voices and meanings, and to the need for dialogue and discussion as an integral part of a responsive and ethical organizational culture.

Responsibility is one of those key words in management: managers are responsible for achieving goals by the most effective and efficient means possible, for managing budgets, etc. This corresponds to the idea of the manager as rational agent, responsible for work outcomes and for the job performance of subordinates. Rational constructions of responsibility are couched in such a way that they often lead to feelings of liability – that as a manager I have a legal responsibility to make sure the work gets done, my employees work in a safe environment, and so on, because if I don't there will be consequences I'll have to face. This doesn't necessarily give me a personal sense of responsibility as a manager, but rather a duty of responsibility – something I'm obliged to do. But I have been using the term responsibility in a different sense: one that focuses on the *response* part of the word and one that offers a very different way of thinking about who we are and what we say and do as managers.

In Chapter 2 we talked about relationally-*respons*ive dialogue and how our everyday conversations entail an intuitive as well as a more deliberate *respons*iveness to the words, gestures and feelings of others; which means that we have a responsibility to consider and *respond* to others – *to be responsive, responsible and accountable to others in our everyday interactions with them*. This reconstruction of power and responsibility emphasizes their embedded and relational nature. Responsibility is not just something that is formalized or legalized in specific items identified on a job description or in policy and procedure documents, but situated in our everyday relationships – in which we are responsible to and with others. Contrast also the language 'responsible for …' and 'responsible to and with …'. The latter implies we can't avoid responsibility because it's implicit in our interactions with other people. Avoiding responsibility means denying the very sociality of our existence, because everything we say and do is in relation to others. So, as we interact, we have a responsibility to each other, to listen, to consider and to respond in appropriate and respectful ways.

This way of thinking about responsibility is crucial to managing communities of difference in relational, reflexive and ethical ways because it means thinking about how our assumptions influence what we say or might not say, and how others might respond. As we will see in the next chapter, it draws on existential and phenomenological conceptions. It is also interwoven with identity-work because when Sartre says we are 'condemned to be free' (1956: 529) he is arguing it is so because we are responsible for making choices about who we are and what we do, and that we also have a responsibility for others. In those choices lie both uncertainties and opportunities to realize our being and our sense of self. Life is not easy.

So can we shape responsive and ethical organizational cultures, where people are not marginalized and where differences are respected? Let's take Mike Agar's notion of culture as difference and Bakhtin's notion of language and dialogism and see what they might have to offer us in terms of managing organizations in this way. If we accept the ideas presented in Chapter 2 that we dialectically shape our social realities and that language is crucial to this process, then we can reframe organizational culture as constantly emerging relational communities of difference created and maintained in our everyday interactions and conversations.

But what might this look like? The notion of polyphony is one often taken up by feminist scholars concerned with different ways of managing and organizing; where dialogue and polyphony are seen as participation, minimizing rules and maximizing personal choice, and offering options rather than instructions. Karen Ashcraft's (2001a, 2001b) study of an organization run by women for battered women found that even though a formal hierarchical structure existed on paper, power relationships were minimized in favour of empowerment. Rules were kept to essential concerns (such as client confidentiality), power relations still existed but attempts to balance these were made by using 'we' (rather than 'I') and by aiming for consensus. This was supported by a D/discourse of *ethical communication* in which the goal was both client and employee empowerment – to reach mutual agreement between different and equal employee voices, through open, straight and collaborative communication. Each employee had a personal responsibility to express her thoughts, feelings and ideas, and to be sensitive to the emotions of others. This was not a perfect world, there were problems, but these ideals were worked upon every day. This process of what Ashcraft calls *relational sensemaking* is also, I suggest, an example of responsive responsibility in which differences are recognized, heard, respected and built upon ... Bakhtin's notion of dialogism.

## Summary

In this chapter we've built on the two key premises of the previous chapters, that managing is both a relational and a dialectical practice in the sense that managers, along with other members of the organization, shape and maintain 'organizational culture' in their everyday interactions and conversations. From a critical perspective, managing organizational culture is not as benign a process as we might think, people can be silenced and made invisible because of monologic values and practices.

Relational, reflexive and ethical managers are attuned to the heteroglossic and polyphonic nature of organizational culture, to:

- how people experience organizational life in similar and different ways
- different and competing voices
- different interpretations of texts, symbols, events and actions
- what is said as well as the silences
- what employees feel cannot be said
- and to the impact of monologic ways of talking and acting.

They manage culture in relational, reflexive and ethical ways by moving beyond control, colonization and minimizing difference, towards Agar's idea of *acculturation*, relating across difference and the many individual voices in our community and conversations. By figuring out how we connect and how we differ, we can employ that 'free speech plan' and build on the connections and differences to remain distinct and yet changed in some way. Understanding culture as difference offers opportunities for managing people and organizations in more responsive and ethical ways, and reframes managing as relational and managers as cultural explorers and adventurers rather than manipulators.

### Notes

1. The Free Dictionary, wwwthefreedictionary.com/cult (accessed 11 July 2013).
2. www.time.com/time/magazine/article/0,9171,1001826-2,00.html (accessed 30 July 2008).
3. www.guardian.co.uk/commentisfree/2012/jun/30/vince-cable-banking-scandal-coalition (accessed 4 September 2013).
4. www.microsoft.com/uk/careers/values.mspx (accessed 19 September 2008).
5. See Borofsky (2005) for a discussion of the controversy and its implications.
6. *Wall Street Journal*, 20 February 2002.
7. See Cunliffe and Eriksen (2011).
8. www.the-storytellers.com (accessed 15 July 2013).
9. http://www.tompeters.com/docs/leadership.reductionist.0719.13.pdf (accessed 4 September 2013).
10. See: www.fawcettsociety.org.uk/wp-content/uploads/2013/02/Sex-and-Power-2013-FINAL-REPORT.pdf; www.ons.gov.uk/ons/rel/ashe/annual-survey-of-hours-and-earnings/2012-provisional-results/stb-ashe-statistical-bulletin-2012.html; www.wgea.gov.au/sites/default/files/2012_CENSUS%20REPORT.pdf (all accessed 12 September 2013).
11. www.youtube.com/watch?v=g-IrhRSwF9U&eurl=http://www.salon.com/mwt/broadsheet/feature/2008/05/27/sexism_sells/ (accessed 4 September 2014).
12. www.newyorker.com/online/blogs/newsdesk/2012/10/julia-gillards-misogyny-speech.html (accessed 4 September 2013).
13. http://storymakerplc.yolasite.com/reflective-conversation.php (accessed 15 July 2013)

# 5

# Managing Ethical and 'Just' Organizations

> Ethical intention [is] aiming at the 'good life' with and for
> others, in just institutions. (Ricoeur, 1992: 172)

In 2011, Antoine Zacharias, ex CEO of French construction company Vinci, was convicted of misusing company funds – a criminal abuse of power – after he received a pay and retirement package of around £90 million. He sacked remuneration committee members who refused to approve his pay request, appointing new members who did approve the package. It was also claimed that he lavishly renovated the Chairman's town house.

I want to begin this final chapter by saying that I'm a moral optimist. I believe fundamentally that people are good and that we can live well together. Yes, we make mistakes and people are going to let you down. Yes, evil exists. Yes, as we see in the example of Zacharias (above) and examples to follow, managers and employees act in unethical and self-interested ways. And yes, organizations can be pathological in that conflict, alienation, discrimination, bullying and other inequities exist. But the point of this chapter is that if we don't believe we can act in morally good ways and create an organizational life characterized by ethical and just behaviour, then we are never going to change anything. The alternative readings of managing and managers that I've offered in previous chapters all lead up to the main point of this chapter: *that managers are responsible for managing in ethical and moral ways and for creating responsive, ethical and 'just' organizations.* This is the ultimate goal of Critical Management Studies, to advocate more humane, socially responsible and just forms of managing and organizing. For some scholars, the answer is authentic leadership (e.g., Petit and Bollaert, 2012), but I suggest that leaders and managers also need a deeper reflexive, relational and ethical understanding of who they are in the world and what responsibilities this brings. So the purpose of this chapter is to explore what this might mean, and in particular to take Ricoeur's notion of ethical intention and relate it to managing organizations.

I draw on Ricoeur's work particularly because he views ethics and morality as both interpersonal and institutional, and there are two main implications that we will examine throughout this chapter:

1. That each of us takes responsibility for acting in ethical ways as well as ensuring that equity, morality and justice exist at an organizational level.
2. That institutional codes of ethics alone are not enough to ensure people act in ethical ways.

In other words, managers have both a personal and an institutional responsibility to act in ethical ways. There's a danger, when studying ethics, in looking purely at moral theory without embedding it in practice, or looking at a moral practice (for example, examining case studies of ethical dilemmas) uninformed by theory. Canadian political and moral philosopher Charles Taylor argues that we need to examine the relationship between moral theory, common understandings and background practices. He uses the term *social imaginary* to describe the latter:

> Something much broader and deeper than the intellectual schemes people may entertain when they think about social reality in a disengaged mode. I am thinking, rather, of the ways people imagine their social existence, how they fit together with others, how things go on between them and their fellows, the expectations that are normally met, and the deeper normative notions and images that underlie these expectations. (2004: 23)

I want to suggest that an understanding of our background practices – our everyday relationally-responsive interaction – is crucial to managing in ethical ways: *that we need to consider the moral social imaginaries within organizational life and the responsibilities these bring for managers*. This is where Ricoeur's ideas meet the idea of managing as relational, reflexive and ethical, and offer a way forward ... for he believes ethics (being a good person) and morality (moral laws and the rule of justice) are interwoven.

We'll begin this chapter by looking at some of the current issues relating to business ethics, and then move on to explore Ricoeur's ideas and their implications for managing organizations in ethical and moral ways.

## What is ethics?

> Ethics? I suppose the most common definition of ethics is the attempt to build a systematic set of normative prescriptions about human behaviour, codes to govern everyday morals and morality. (Parker, 1998: 1)

There is a plethora of journal articles and books on ethics, including religious, philosophical, political, academic and professional texts. Yet despite this, or perhaps because of it, there is still much debate on what ethics is, should be and should do; about whether we can identify universal ethical norms; about whose ethical principles are the correct ones (as the saying goes, 'one person's terrorist is another person's freedom fighter'); and about whether ethical prescriptions influence practice. I discovered an article written in 1911 by George Adams, who argues that religion and metaphysics just aren't enough, because they define absolute ideals and truths rather than focus on common sense or practical life. He says that we need to be concerned with 'the humbler task of the organization of our social experience, the relief of poverty, the freeing of human life everywhere from the obstructions which greed and ignorance impose, – with acting everywhere in the light of ideals wholly relative to the best we know and can do' (1911: 229). And I agree with him. Having moral ideals and laws in place is fine, but ethics is essentially about human behaviour and practical action: about how we treat each other in our everyday interactions in organizations and in society at large.

There are a number of major debates in philosophical ethics, one of which is that of moral universalism versus moral relativism. The meaning of these terms can be debated, so let me frame this debate as one between those who believe that morality is grounded in universal laws, values, principles and a system of ethics, which apply to everyone everywhere (often equated with universalism), and those who believe that morality is grounded in the actual relationships we live out with one another (often equated with relativism). The former view relates to the idea that there are human rights fundamental to all people, regardless of where they live. The 1948 Universal Declaration of Human Rights addresses those rights; for example, Article 4 states that: 'No one shall be held in slavery or servitude; slavery and the slave trade shall be prohibited in all their forms'. Those who believe morality is grounded in relationships claim that moral values are culturally influenced and therefore moral judgements are subjective. If we place this debate within a business context, it is perhaps best illustrated by the issue of what constitutes bribery. In the USA, it's a crime to use money or other forms of payoffs to win business both at home and overseas. Yet what may be constituted as a bribe in one country might be seen as an accepted social norm of gift-giving in another. And to partly counter the difficulties associated with these differences, the WTO (World Trade Organization) and OECD (Organization for Economic Cooperation and Development) address international anti-bribery by establishing common agreements – conventions that are enforceable by law. There are also a number of non-profit organizations such as Global Integrity and Transparency International which investigate and report on global corruption and transparency. You can check their websites for reports on the performance of various countries.

Another debate centres on the issue of whether ethical laws and prescriptions influence practice. Despite having laws and ethical codes of conduct, corruption, fraud and other forms of ethical misconduct are still prevalent in organizations. Un/ethical misconduct relates to un/ethical cultures and the behaviour of individual organizational members, sometimes individual employees – for example, Barings Bank collapsed in 1995 because of the actions of individual rogue trader Nick Leeson – but most often managers. In 1991 the Luxembourg Bank of Credit and Commerce International was closed. An investigation by the US Justice Department stated that the bank's officers 'were sophisticated international bankers whose apparent objective was to keep their affairs secret, to commit fraud on a massive scale, and to avoid detection' (Henderson, 2002: 273). This is perhaps a grim reminder of Stein's (2011) argument that leaders and managers may engage in manic denial.

And the list of corporate malfeasance goes on ...

At a corporate level, one of the most recent ethical scandals is the massive Libor (London Interbank Offered Rate) fixing scandal that came to light in 2012. Banks were manipulating Libor rates (the rate at which London banks make short-term loans) to benefit themselves. This had a negative impact on individual customers who took out loans and on the financial market as a whole. Barclays Bank admitted misconduct and paid fines of around £290m and the chairman and CEO resigned. Swiss Bank UBS were also fined £940m by US, UK and Swiss regulators, the Royal Bank of Scotland paid £390m and Deutsche Bank is currently awaiting a settlement with authorities of an estimated €500m.

Yet these banks have codes of ethics. Barclays, for example, has policies on bribery and corruption and an eight-page code of corporate conduct and ethics.[1] So why aren't ethical codes of conduct and training enough? Is it that managing and ethics are a contradiction in terms? Is it a case of 'do as I say not as I do'? Or is there a conflict between what it means to be a good person, a good employee and a good manager – between personal and professional ethics, loyalty and morality? Employees face moral dilemmas every day. One example from my own experience comes to mind: I was instructed to carry out an act I knew was illegal under the threat of being ostracized because I was not being a 'team player'. I didn't comply, and it may be just coincidental that I was soon after passed over for promotion. Is it that we somehow don't get the balance right between universal ideals and individual responsibility?

Robert Jackall's classic 1988 study of managerial life in corporate America, *Moral Mazes*, focuses on the moral rules-in-use managers employ in day-to-day operations. He argues that managers hold a pivotal institutional and social position because 'their occupational ethics and the way they come to see the world set both the frameworks and the vocabularies for a great many public issues in our society' (1988: 12). Yet despite this position, he found managers were not subject to universal moral truths, rather needing to be alert to their organizational requirements and to expediency, the 'ideological idols of the moment' (1988: 133). In doing so, they viewed relationships in a strictly utilitarian way, while continually assessing the moral fitness of their colleagues. He suggests that moral actions of managers are influenced by organizational criteria of 'success', by how one has to prove one's worth and by the moral viewpoints and methodological rationalities of bureaucracies. This is still evident today in the scandals I've noted. In other words, managers are subject to moral relativism.

Yet can employees report illegal and immoral actions (whistleblowing) in their organization? This is a timely issue ... Edward Snowden, an analyst employed by a defence contractor for the US National Security Agency leaked information about alleged mass citizen surveillance programmes in the USA, UK and France, aided by Australia and New Zealand. He is currently (July 2013) seeking political asylum in Russia, charged with espionage. This situation is an interesting contrast to Norway, where one study found that 78 per cent of public employees reported some sort of misconduct to someone in their organization (Skivenes and Trygstad, 2010). In 83 per cent of these cases, whistleblowers reported receiving a positive response.

One argument for the failure of ethical codes of practice is that such codes can actually encourage employees to cheat, because they give the cheaters a competitive advantage over others. In the US, a person can file a Qui Tam lawsuit in the name of the US government, claiming fraud by government contractors – and receive a share of the recovered money. One could take a cynical perspective and argue that the longer the whistleblower keeps quiet before reporting any such activity, the bigger the payout. This argument about encouraging cheating also relates to industry codes and international agreements, which depend on all organizations sticking to the agreement. The violation of a code, let's say anti-bribery, by one organization can give that organization a huge competitive advantage. So opposing pressures can exist for both conformity and nonconformity, and it's important to consider what those might be and to try to anticipate and minimize the counter-pressures to ethical action. *Moral communities are created by the beliefs, values, actions and commitments of individual members of that moral community.*

Furthermore, as we saw in Chapter 3, the various conceptualizations of managers have implications for how we view ethics. For example, rational managers will probably work from an enlightened perspective by engaging in objective moral reflection and reasoned action to the benefit of the 'common' good. But as we have seen, what constitutes rationality and the common good is open to interpretation and is a political process based on self and/or group interests. Managers as actors may engage in performances that have ethical implications because they are aimed at manipulating other actors or other performances. Managers as discursively constructed subjects may find themselves struggling with ethical dilemmas as they are subject to control or marginalization by various discourses. Managers of meaning are concerned with creating credible stories with a moral plot. For example, Andrea Whittle and Frank Mueller (2012) studied the moral stories constructed during a UK public hearing on the financial crisis. In particular they looked at how the moral character of participants (bankers and regulators) was constructed. They found two storylines: a tragic story with bankers as villains, created by committee members, and an epic story with bankers as victims, created by the bankers. Finally, relational and reflexive managers recognize that being always in-relation with others means that they have an ethical responsibility to those others, that they need to reveal unethical cultures and actions and remedy them.

The Enron case reinforces the crucial role that managers play in creating and maintaining both unethical and ethical cultures. It also highlights that organizational ethics is complex and is, as Robert Jackall says, a moral maze with multi-dimensional aspects, competing pressures and various interpretations of what might be reasonable and ethical depending on whose point of view. The classic example of a moral maze can be seen in the 1987 Challenger Shuttle disaster, and the various pressures experienced by Morton-Thiokol managers and engineers during a 1987 teleconference with NASA and the Marshall Space Flight Center about whether it was safe to launch. After recommending not to launch the shuttle at temperatures below 53 degrees Fahrenheit, Morton-Thiokol senior managers and engineers, feeling under pressure by NASA to justify their decision with data they couldn't produce, had an off-line discussion. At one point during the discussion, the general manager says, 'Take off your engineering hat and put on your management hat'. This simple statement reframed the issues under consideration from a technical decision to a political one of meeting customer requirements, and changed the vote to a recommendation to launch with no additional technical data.[2] I still use this example because although it is over 20 years old, it is a compelling illustration of both the power of language and the importance of taking a moral stance.

Can we take anything from the literature and from business experience that might be helpful in managing organizations in ethical and socially responsible ways?

### Ethics and managing

Today, business ethics is part of most management education programmes and is a legitimate concern of society at large because business decisions affect individuals, communities and our environment. As a topic of study, business ethics addresses a number of issues, including the ethical nature of capitalism, the ability of business ethics to impact business in practice, the challenges of meeting all stakeholder demands in responsible and ethical ways, corporate governance practices, and the role of moral reflection and debate. Three issues stand out:

1. corporate social responsibility and sustainable development
2. business ethics
3. ethical management.

### Corporate social responsibility (CSR) and sustainable development

CSR addresses a number of moral issues relating to an organization's role in and responsibility for environmental degradation, global warming, worldwide poverty, child labour, community sustainability and politically correct accounting/marketing. Back in 1995, Arturo Escobar argued from a poststructuralist discursive perspective that development is 'a historical construct that provides a space in which poor countries are known, specified, and intervened upon' (1995: 45). This is reinforced by a 'top-down, ethnocentric and technocratic approach, which treated people and cultures as abstract concepts [and] statistical figures' (1995: 44). So companies treat CSR and sustainability as some*thing* to be managed to ensure economic growth rather than environmental sustainability. For example, if poverty is constructed from a westernized corporate perspective, it can be alleviated by providing employment and contracting out operations to poor countries – where employees get paid a below minimum wage. A lengthy discussion on this complex issue is not within the purview of this book, but check Winn and Pogutz (2013) who consider a number of issues that managers and management research need to address in this area.

A number of organizations identify core CSR and environmental sustainability values. One example is the UK-based Co-operative Bank, which runs TV adverts stating that they do not invest in oppressive regimes or businesses who supply arms, and that they refuse loans to companies who act in conflict with the Co-op's ethical policy. They encourage members to stand up for human rights.[3] You might also want to look at the Ethisphere list of the world's most ethical companies, which ranks companies on issues such as: ethics and compliance; reputation, leadership and innovation; governance; corporate citizenship and responsibility; and a culture of ethics. In 2013, the top three companies are Asea Brown Boveri Ltd (Switzerland), Accenture (Ireland) and Adobe Systems Incorporated (USA).[4]

CSR recognizes an issue we discussed in Chapter 1, the pivotal role managers and organizations play in society today and a manager's responsibility to the community at large.

## Business ethics

A second issue is business ethics, which focuses on the development of codes of ethics and ethical frameworks relating to workplace issues and employer–employee relationships. Over the last 10 years, business ethics has become part of many management education programmes, sometimes drawing on philosophy, contrasting the utilitarian ethics of Hobbes (1651), Bentham (1789) and Mill (1861) with the duty ethics of Kant (1785) and Rawls (1971). While *utilitarian ethics* advocates that the enlightened and educated mind judges actions by their consequences, for example, as Bentham argued, the greatest good/happiness for the greatest number, *duty ethics* focuses on the inherent rightness and wrongness of actions and the motivation behind such actions and decisions. In order to make a point, although risking oversimplification, utilitarian ethics is perhaps best (although ironically!) captured in the notion that '*ethics pays*'! In other words, that being seen to be ethical both looks good and is good for business because it maximizes profit – which ultimately benefits everyone. This instrumental notion of ethics encourages conformity and obedience rather than a reflexive questioning of the fundamental responsibilities of business and the wider social impact of managerial decision-making. Indeed, as Hugh Willmott (1998) says, it can be seen as just another way of controlling employee behaviour towards organizational values and interests.

Within duty ethics, Immanuel Kant argued that we understand our experience through innate knowledge that helps us organize what's happening around us. He assumed that morality is related to rational beings accepting and acting upon universal law, and argued that we should act out of respect for moral law rather than self-interest – and a moral law is good if it is able to withstand contradiction. His famous dictum – 'Always treat humanity, whether in yourself or in other people, as an end in itself and never as a mere means' – still stands the test of time today. John Rawls offers an example of moral universalism because he provides a *theory of justice* that says a moral law can be valid if generalized to everyone, and to do so we have to use what he calls an imaginative device – to put ourselves in a neutral position behind a veil of ignorance, then to imagine what a just world would look like. This gives a basis for articulating what is just, and for providing criteria against which we measure existing institutions. To do so, Rawls argues that we need to completely abstract ourselves from the actual social world – a totally opposite view to that of Charles Taylor's social imaginaries, which emphasizes an implicit grasp or sense of moral order lying within our everyday practice. And, as I have asked in previous chapters, when can we ever be neutral? Neutrality and abstraction imply a god-like being, with no history or biography, someone who exists outside a social context with his or her own particular ways of thinking and acting ... and I haven't met anyone like that! But an absence of neutrality shouldn't surely prevent managers from working within the polyphony of social experience, recognizing that there are different views but that we can sit down and come to some agreement about what a just organization should be?

### Ethical management

Ethical management and leadership defines and examines the core principles and virtues central to ethical and more democratic management of organizations. A major aspect of this work is *virtue ethics*, which goes back to Aristotle and Plato who argued that ethics relates to the character and motives of people: we do what is right because we are virtuous. Virtue ethics is about living our lives in purposeful and virtuous ways. For Aristotle, this meant achieving *phronêsis*, the practical wisdom or prudence necessary to enhance our happiness and quality of life. A number of well-known leaders are hailed for their philanthropy. Bill Gates, co-founder of Microsoft, established the Bill and Melinda Gates Foundation in 2000, with a $27 billion endowment dedicated to reducing inequities around the world. But philanthropic management also exists at the local level. For example, one large car dealership in New Mexico has a free on-site nurse and 24-hour clinic for employees and their families, and is one of the few car dealerships that closes on Sundays because of the owner's view that Sunday is family time. For the owner, this is not a question of profit, but of 'running my business the right way'. A number of senior managers I know talk about the importance of having a person within and outside of the organization who will listen, question and act as a moral compass for them. Someone who, as one manager commented:

> holds me accountable for my actions, and also challenges my thinking in a way that no one else has ever done before. He models for me the value of servant-leadership and also integrity in character. He tries to stretch me beyond myself, beyond my normal methods of operating and thinking, by challenging my assumptions. (Duffy Swan, Chairman, French Funerals)

## Feminist ethics

Over the last 15 years, feminist ethics has offered an alternative way of thinking about ethics and management. Lawrence Kohlberg (1969), whose work was initially based on Rawls's theory of justice, identified six stages of moral reasoning through which he believed we must move if we are to become more morally and socially responsible. His work is often used in business ethics programmes to teach students how to become moral agents. In *In a Different Voice*, Carol Gilligan (1982) argued that Kohlberg's work was gender biased because his studies were only of men and he assumed that the moral thinking of males would be representative of all humanity. Men scored higher on questionnaires relating to the model, and Kohlberg argued that women were lower on the scale of moral development than men because they didn't move past Stage 3 of the model. Gilligan suggested that the moral reasoning of women is different from men in that women emphasize care, trust, mutuality and responsibility, in other words, relationships rather than rights and justice. So rather than working from a morality of justice based on the injunction not to hurt others, women work from a morality of care, which means acting responsively to others.

Even though Gilligan is careful to argue that both are valid modes of understanding, her work has been criticized by some feminist scholars such as Judith Butler, who argue that feminist ethics reinforces the gender stereotyping and oppression of women as underpaid carers, and emphasizes the division between public (organizational) and private (caring family) life. Nevertheless, Gilligan's work has been instrumental in drawing attention to the careless use of one voice – the patriarchal voice – that is so pervasive and powerful in the realm of theory and practice. And she shifted attention from an abstract, universal and dispassionate consideration of individual rights and ethics, to a relational voice and connectedness – the need to consider our primary ethical responsibility for others in actual circumstances. Whether we agree or disagree that the moralities of justice and care follow gender demarcation, her belief that sensitivity to human relationships is central to moral understanding is an important way of viewing the ethical responsibilities of managers. And a relational voice takes on very practical connotations through the following evocative comment:

> Listening to human voices, Noel finds that one voice, speaking in a particular emotional register can stop the emotional vibrations in a group of people so that the environment in the room becomes deadened or flat. When this happens, she observes, it looks like silence but in fact the feelings and thoughts – the psychological energy – often move into the only place they can still live, and vibrate in silence, in the inner sense, until it becomes possible to bring them back into the world ...[5]

Have you ever sat in a meeting and felt the 'deadening' of the conversation after someone speaks? Where, based on what one person has said or how they've said it, other participants feel that their voice will not be heard and so remain silent? In this instance, dialogue becomes a monologue. This has real implications for the way we interact and relate with others in personal and organizational settings.

A feminist ethics of care plays through Joan Acker's notion of the non-responsibility of work organizations. She argues that within western society, economic organizations are privileged over other forms of life. Many organizations are characterized by non-responsibility, 'refusals or attempts to avoid contributions to meeting the needs of people, if these contributions do not directly enhance production or accumulation' (Acker, 2005: 94). She frames her argument by saying that economic activity is about the processes of *provisioning* – providing the necessities of community and survival through reproduction – and *production*, which is about profit. In capitalist societies, the focus is on the latter, on 'rational economic man' and the rational manager. The production process is not just one of unequal power, it's gendered (because women are mainly involved in provisioning and in the unpaid work of caring and reproduction), racialized (racial and ethnic minorities often occupy low-paid, menial jobs), and class-based because working-class jobs often don't incorporate provisioning needs. This leads to what she calls the non-responsibility of capitalist organizations for meeting the provisioning needs of society, particularly in relation to issues of minimum wage, pay equity, benefits, quality day-care, family leave, work–life balance, product safety and environmental and community responsibility.

Businesses often do not consider or act on these issues until forced to by legislation and, as Acker says, the ideal employee is often seen to be the person without family or community obligations. Employees often face career choices in which the work expectations associated with advancement have serious consequences for life outside work. And while this has negative consequences for both men and women, women are mainly affected because they are traditionally responsible for caring. Acker suggests that we need to redefine the process of production and the organization of work to value and support both work and family. Of course, many businesses resist this because they think it has a negative impact on profitability. But would you be committed to, and want to stay with, an organization that requires you to work 60 hours a week with below minimum pay? Should employers have a duty of care for the mental and physical health of their employees? Sweden, for example, has generous parental leave benefits: 240 days per parent, of which 80 per cent are paid; flexible work arrangements; and sabbatical leave for employees.

## Can managers be ethical?

There is debate around whether management and ethics are a contradiction in terms. Cynics argue that management, ethics and morality don't go together because managers have to act on behalf of owners and shareholders rather than the common good. So, in the interest of efficiency and profit, managers have to view people as instrumental – objects or assets to be manipulated like any other material resource. Moral and political philosopher Alasdair MacIntyre, whose work explores the relationship between morality, culture and politics, argues this view eloquently. A central theme in his work is that modern life lacks a moral code and civility and that this needs to change. In his 1981 book, *After Virtue*, he considers the moral inconsistencies within society, and how we often justify our actions and preferences by using the language of reason and morality. Two particular issues are relevant to our discussion of management.

First, MacIntyre argues controversially that morality in today's world is characterized by emotivism, the idea that moral judgements are not based on universal criteria but are expressions of preference and self-interest in which we try to obtain our goals by persuasion and by emotional appeals. Thus, we are always trying to gain power over others – just as they are trying to gain power over us. Does this mean that people who are good at manipulating others, who desire power, who are self-interested and who treat people as means not ends, are those who become leaders? MacIntyre believes so, for as he famously declares, the barbarians have been governing us for some time ([1981] 2007: 263)! And if this is so, what does this mean for civilized and just organizations?

Second, he describes managers as 'characters', representatives of modern culture and its moral ideals. Characters are clusters of moral beliefs, activities and attitudes that legitimate a way of being and acting. For MacIntyre, the problem lies in the idea that managers are perceived as engaging in value-neutral activities that are concerned with rational and efficient means rather than ends. This is reinforced through language that frames people as objects: as assets, costs and benefits. As a result, people are ignored, as managers (knowingly or otherwise) manipulate others to achieve organizational goals. The irony lies in our seeing ourselves as moral agents: we think we are autonomous, free, that there are self-evident truths, and that we do not manipulate others, nor are we manipulated by them. But we do and are! He argues that managers justify their authority by claiming they have the skills and expertise to make the organization effective and efficient. But, he asks, 'What if effectiveness is part of a masquerade of social control rather than a reality?' ... because the kind of knowledge that sustains such expertise is 'one more moral fiction' ([1981] 2007: 75).

The managers in Robert Jackall's study in a way recognized this fiction: one former vice president in the study commented, *'What is right in the corporation is what the guy above you wants from you. That's what morality is in the corporation'* (1988: 6). Executive and business school programmes offering more efficient ways of achieving organizational goals maintain this moral fiction by teaching rational management techniques and egocentric and heroic approaches to leadership, which focus on confident action rather than a moral debate on goals or social responsibility. A critical evaluation of ends is generally not part of the curriculum. Managers are exhorted 'To boldly go where no man has gone before' – as embodied in the famously declared *Star Trek* Enterprise mission statement. (An aside: it seems the criticisms of the 1960's Captain Kirk heroic gendered leadership style and the portrayal of women have not been addressed in the latest 2013 Star Trek film.)

As Sumantra Ghoshal states, 'By propagating ideologically inspired amoral theories, business schools have actively freed their students from any sense of moral responsibility' (2005: 76). If we frame ethics as part of this moral fiction of rationality and neutrality, then we should be able to develop an ethical algorithm that eliminates moral debate and gives us a logical answer to any ethical dilemma ... and such algorithms do exist!

I've found that MacIntyre's ideas about management often cause much debate, and sometimes denial, among students – but consider a comment made in a paper written by a manager in my class a few years ago:

> My initial role was that of an operations analysis manager. In simpler terms I performed statistical analysis and mathematical modeling to justify the Assistant General Manager's decisions to reduce workforce and require his management staff to do more with less. In this role I was the essence of bureaucratic rationality 'the rationality of matching means to ends economically and efficiently' (MacIntyre, 1981: 25). Further I can honestly confess that consistent to the character of a manager described by MacIntyre, I was not 'engaged in moral debate'. My work was used directly in justifying over 300 layoffs and countless sleepless nights for other managers who had to figure out how to deliver on ever increasing service standards, with higher revenue and transactions, while having less labor. While performing this I never concerned myself with the moral implications of such work, rather I took great pride in 'technique, with effectiveness in transforming ... investment into profits' (MacIntyre, [1981] 2007: 30).

This is part of the taken-for-granted nature of management that we discussed in previous chapters, and of the idea that managers themselves are victims of the logic of managerialism: subject to the pressures to produce and to act 'rationally' and be rewarded for doing so. 'Increasingly, managers are the victims and not just the agents of a rationality that inhibits critical reflection upon, and transformation of, a structure of social relations that systematically impedes and distorts efforts to develop more ethically rational, morally defensible forms of management theory and practice' (Alvesson and Willmott, 1996: 36).

This all sounds rather cynical, overly critical and depressing. Are managers really just morally neutral technicians? Do managers engage in moral debate? Are organizations doomed to be pathological or can they be different? These questions highlight the moral complexities of management and of organizational life. As individuals, we face moral choices because 'what is right' is interpreted in various ways, and in organizations we find ourselves coping with many different pressures and having to answer to various 'stakeholders' – but ultimately to ourselves. This is where I turn to phenomenology and Ricoeur's work ...

## Moral managers

### Phenomenology and ethics

> Existentialism's first move is to make every man aware of what he is and to make the full responsibility of his existence rest on him. And when we say that a man is responsible for himself, we do not only mean that he is responsible for his own individuality, but that he is responsible for all men. (Sartre, 1956: 36)

We began this book by drawing on a philosophical understanding, and I'm returning to philosophy in this final chapter. While there's a general assumption that philosophy is about very abstract and esoteric issues, there are many aspects that address serious and practical issues about the way we live our lives. Philosophy and, in particular, phenomenology speak to ethics because they give us a context in which to situate and question our beliefs about the way the world works, about the nature of knowledge and about who we are. They also, as in the quote by Sartre above, address our responsibility for others. And while most managers ordinarily don't have time to sit down and read philosophical texts, I've found that when they do, they find some intriguing and useful ideas. Let me set the scene by sketching the main concerns of phenomenology.

Phenomenology explores the relationship between ourselves and our lived experience, or, in phenomenological terms, our *life-world*. We can trace its roots back to the work of Husserl, Sartre, Heidegger and to some of the authors we've mentioned previously, namely Merleau-Ponty and Ricoeur. Although there are different approaches to phenomenology, the unifying theme is a concern about viewing the world in terms of 'things' and objects: as abstract representations such as systems, models, laws and categories. For phenomenologists, objects and events only gain meaning as we encounter them in human consciousness; they do not have meaning independent of our perception. If we look back to Chapters 1 and 3 at the various ways in which managerial identity has been theorized, you may note it has most frequently been framed in generalized object-oriented ways, for example, managers as rational agents, actors or discursive subjects. Think about management and leadership courses you may have attended where you have completed self-assessment and personality questionnaires to discover what type of manager or leader you are. Such instruments provide generalized social categories such as introvert or extrovert, people- or task-oriented, transformative or transactional, etc., against which we can compare ourselves. And here lies a fundamental issue, because phenomenologists, in particular Sartre, Merleau-Ponty and Ricoeur, suggest that thinking about ourselves purely in terms of such external referents and general social categories strips us of our humanness, and turns us into objects separate from our everyday lived experience. Thinking about ourselves as a 'what' (as 'the management', 'a rational manager', an 'introvert') removes any sense of responsibility for our actions and for our relationships with others. We take these categorizations for granted and we don't engage in a critical questioning of our actions.

Briefly, Husserl's work on transcendental phenomenology was concerned with how the world appears to us through our perception or imagination; with studying the true nature or *essence* of something by *bracketing experience*, for example, examining the structure and properties of consciousness while suspending questions and beliefs about the nature of the world (see, for example, Husserl, 1983). So Husserl's phenomenology involved studying how we come to know phenomena (objects and events) through a disembodied consciousness. His ideas provided inspiration for a number of scholars, who went on to develop variations of phenomenology, including Sartre, whose work is often regarded as the cornerstone of *existential phenomenology*, and Ricoeur, who developed an approach to phenomenology he called *hermeneutic phenomenology*.

Existential phenomenologists such as Sartre and Heidegger are more concerned with the nature of being *in the lived world*. Sartre (1956), for example, suggests that *being* is becoming, that human nature isn't fixed: at first we are nothing and we make ourselves who we are by imagining who we will be. Thus, we are 'condemned to be free' (1956: 529) because we are responsible for making choices about who we are and what to do – and in those choices lie both uncertainties and opportunities to realize our being. An awareness of these opportunities and possibilities constitutes one aspect of *being*, that is *being-for-itself* – a self-conscious reflective person. A second aspect, *being-in-itself*, Sartre claims just *is* – is our lives, who we are, pre-conscious and acting instinctively. A third aspect is that of *non-being* or *nothingness*. Sartre captures the relationship between being and nothingness when he argues that I am not the self I will be, because there are infinite possibilities and choices in between who I am and who I will become. Who we are will always be open because we are both pre-reflectively and self-reflectively embedded in the phenomenological moment of experience. What this means is that our personal and work identities are fluid. We are constantly expressing and figuring out who we are in our everyday experience as we interact with others and make choices about what to do.

However, I believe it is hermeneutic phenomenology that offers a number of connections and insights for managers and leaders, because this version of phenomenology addresses issues of relationality, identity, critical reflection and ethics (Cunliffe, 2009). Not only is identity reflective and fluid, as Sartre suggests, but it's also socially embedded. Hermeneutics is about interpretation, and hermeneutic phenomenology addresses the interpretive nature of experience, identity and awareness. Ricoeur captures this succinctly when he says that our lives and our selves are an 'unending work of interpretation' (1992: 179) as we try to make sense of who we are and what's happening around us in order to make choices and act. Both Merleau-Ponty (1962, 1964) and Ricoeur argue that we cannot put aside, *bracket*, our surroundings, nor can we focus purely on the individual, because we are intersubjective and embodied beings. So whereas Sartre focused on being as a reflective self-conscious individual (an 'I'), Ricoeur and Merleau-Ponty believe we are inseparable from others ('We') and, particularly for Ricoeur, we are moral selves embracing the ethical intention of living a good life with others. This is where his work becomes relevant to managing ethical organizations.

For Ricoeur, knowing ourselves means asking the question, 'Who am I in relation to others?', and this plays out in our everyday interaction. So we figure out who we are through interpretation and relationality, not purely through social categorization. You may see some connections here with Gilligan's notion of the relational voice. But for Ricoeur and Merleau-Ponty relationality, or in their terminology intersubjectivity, is not about two individuals coordinating their actions and coming to an understanding of what the other person thinks – indeed, this would take us back to the traditional communication model in Figure 2.1. Rather, I am who I am because of you – we are inseparable from others because whole parts of our life are part of their life history. Everything we say, think and do is interwoven with particular and generalized others: friends, colleagues, social and professional groups, categories, language systems, culturally and historically situated discursive and non-discursive practices. The *other* is always intertwined with us because we act in a complex web of present and previous relationships, conversations, utterances, language communities, speech genres and historical and cultural ways of speaking (Bakhtin, 1984, 1986). As we saw in Chapter 2, relationality is inherently practical, occurring in our everyday conversations and relationally-responsive interaction, in which everything we do is a complex mixture of our own and others' actions and talk. In these living conversations we are inherently responsive to each other – to our own and others' words, gestures and feelings. Our talk is so interwoven that in our moment-by-moment dialogue no one person is in control. This way of seeing the world means we have a moral responsibility to make available communicative opportunities to talk with, listen to and be responsive to others. It also means we focus on collaborative forms of interacting: on dialogue not monologue, on creating shared meaning between us as we talk, rather than one person persuading the other that their way is the right one.

Okay, so where does this take us in terms of managing organizations in ethical and responsive ways? Summarizing the main themes we've discussed up to this point:

- Codes of ethics only go so far – ethics is about our relationships with others, about how we act and treat others, both particular persons and the wider community.
- Managers are victims of the taken-for-granted notion that rationality, effectiveness and efficiency are neutral concepts, which legitimate their authority – when such concepts and practices are ideologically saturated and sometimes unethical.
- Generalizations and objectifications of self (the 'what') are useful up to a certain point, but can absolve us from ethical responsibility. Discovering 'who' we are can take us towards ethical relationships.
- Ethical action is not about one voice, but recognizing different voices and our responsibility for those voices.
- Ricoeur offers a way for us to think about how we might manage people in ethical ways and create ethical and moral organizations.

Of course, the question is: *how?*

## Ethics and identity-work

In this section we will address the 'how' by examining how ethical action is closely interwoven with who you are – with identity-work. We'll do so by drawing on Ricoeur's work.

In *Oneself as Another* (1992), Ricoeur builds on his earlier work on narrative, interpretation and ethics to explore three key issues. The first is how we can think about identity without losing a sense of self, or who we are, in the process. The second is the relationship between self and ethical intention. The third is how ethical selfhood relates to our broader social and institutional context. What he ends up with is a sort of moral philosophy and moral sociality, because he addresses how moral values and rules play through our relationships and the way we live our lives with others. As in the quote at the beginning of this chapter, he sees ethical intention as '*aiming at the "good life" with and for others, in just institutions*' (1992: 172). How so?

Bear with me a while here – we are going to look at some fairly complex philosophical ideas, but these ideas offer a different way of 'doing' ethics, by offering a way of thinking about how to 'be' ethical. Which resonates with one of the main premises of this book that if we know who we are or who to be – then what to do falls into place. The ideas have some very practical implications for managing organizations. I hope Ricoeurian scholars will forgive my distillation of his complex and nuanced work. Figure 5.1 offers an overview of the ideas we are going to discuss.

Ricoeur suggests we need to consider two modes of being: *idem identity*, that is, concerned with *what* we are; and *ipse selfhood*, that is, concerned with *who* we are. Idem is a Latin term meaning 'the same', so in this sense our identity revolves around how we see ourselves being similar to or the same as others. Sameness is often imputed by generalized character traits (such as introvert, neurotic, emotive) connecting us to others and offering continuity over time and contexts. Ricoeur sees these character traits as the 'what' of identity, because thinking about ourselves in terms of generalized physical

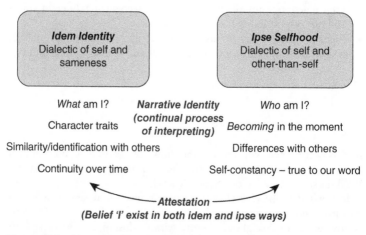

**Figure 5.1**   Narrative identity (after Ricoeur, 1992)

and psychological characteristics turns us into an objectified person, or an individual at large: a combination of physical, mental and social predicates. Ricoeur says this is a 'portrait painted from outside' (1992: 119) and subjects us to already established categories, structures and mechanisms. We can think about the implications of idem identity if we go back to some of the conceptualizations of the role of a manager. If I think about myself as a manager in terms of being a figurehead, monitor, disturbance handler, etc. (Mintzberg, 1973 – see Table 1.1), then I will focus on those actions without necessarily questioning what this means or what the implications might be. There are also often ideal types associated with these generalized character traits, which can have an impact on what we do. For example, let's say you do a personality questionnaire and score highly as a neurotic intro-vert, does that explain who you are and mean that because studies have shown good managers have low scores on neuroticism and are extroverts then you are never going to hack it as a manager? If you think about managers you know and respect, they are not going to have the same personality characteristics. These models are also gen-der and culturally biased – for example, women score higher on neu-roticism. The problem is that we often take idem conceptualizations as givens. And in so doing, we design hiring, performance appraisal, promotion and training programmes around such givens. So there are problems if we think purely in idem terms.

Ricoeur suggests we also need to consider *ipseity*, *ipse* being Latin for self. Ipseity is 'who' we are, our individual self and how we engage with the world. Ipse is about how we are both the same as and different from others, about our uniqueness as individuals. Ricoeur says that ipse emerges in the moments in which we open ourselves to others and find (intuitively and/or explicitly) how we are both similar to and different from others. For Ricoeur, both idem and ipse come together in our everyday interactions as we 'narrate' our sense of identity. What this means practically is that we interpret what is going on, what people are doing and who they are – including ourselves – and we try to create a coherent story about our experience and about what to do.

In a study of Chinese small and medium size business owners and managers in Indonesia, Koning and Waistell (2012) suggest that manag-ers and leaders can 'author' themselves as moral beings by narrating 'their identity work with preferred versions of the self' (2012: 67), i.e., identities they aspire to. Narrating identity is also relational, as one manager com-mented: 'I need to feel that my relation with the workforce is like father to child, I need to give them the good examples but tolerance is needed' (2012: 72). This identity-work is an ongoing process and often a struggle because the managers in the study narrated their ethical identity in a culture where corruption is unquestioned. In other words, their identity-work takes place within broader communities who did not hold similar ideals or norms. As Ricoeur says, we create our narrative identity, an identity that both connects us to, and separates us from, others.

The final piece of the 'identity' puzzle is the notion of *attestation*. Ricoeur says attestation is my ability to see myself as a person in the narrative I'm creating (remember Merleau-Ponty's human dialectic from Chapter 1, the idea that we create the very social realities we think exist separately from us). Attestation means believing that I judge and act well, that I have an ethical intention to lead a good life, and that I can account for myself and my actions to others with conviction. But this does not mean being arrogant enough to believe that every-thing I do is right, ethical selfhood involves an 'uneasy balance between attestation and suspicion' (Ricoeur, 1992: 302) – a balance between believing in myself and questioning myself. In practical terms this is about being self-reflexive, asking:

- Who is speaking?
- Who is acting?
- Who is interpreting?
- How does who I am as a moral person relate to my social surround-ings and the moral norms?

In other words, questioning whether we are speaking and acting in ethical ways, and testing our illusions about ourselves and the meanings of our intentions (Ricoeur, 1992: 240).

A useful way of thinking about this is an idea developed by Chris Argyris and Donald Schön (1974) who talk about the difference between our *espoused theories* (what we say) and our *theories-in-use* (what we do). They make the case that the two should be congruent. However, when asked about how we do something, we give our espoused theory, but the way we actually behave can be very different. I used to run one-day management seminars where participants would say they were definitely participative, but more often than not their immediate response to a short case study about a 'problematic' employee was to fire the person without any conversation with the employee! You might want to check out Argyris's (1991) article, 'Teach-ing smart people how to learn', where he expands on why management consultants and managers engaged in defensive reasoning.

As I was writing the first edition of the book, one of my students sent me a link to a video of US ex-politician John Edwards. Edwards had just been in the news because of his alleged affair with the video's director.[6] In 2011 he was indicted on six felony charges of violating campaign contribution laws in his attempt to cover up an extra-marital affair. The video begins with Edwards saying that he wants the American public to know 'who I really am', and shows him at a political rally saying, 'If we want to live in a moral, honest and just America, if we want to live in a moral and just world, we can't wait for somebody else to do it. We have to do it' – a disconnect between his espoused theory and his theory-in-use! It's interesting that he later says, 'We are conditioned to be political'. Regardless of your politics, the video is a not-to-be-missed example of impression management!

This example also brings us to Ricoeur's notion of ethical intention, which is the core of ethical selfhood because it's at the heart of who we are. He draws upon, and extends, Aristotle's notion of *phronêsis*, the practical wisdom necessary to enhance our happiness and quality of life, arguing that self and moral character are the cornerstones of ethics, as opposed to a moral society and moral norms. My interpretation of this point is that practical wisdom is a common sense and understanding that allow us to make ethical decisions in practical circumstances, without resorting only to universal laws or only to total relativism. And ethical selfhood means:

1. Self-constancy: being true to our word, being capable of evaluating our actions and believing they are ethical and good, and conducting ourselves so others may count on us. As Ricoeur says, '"From you," says the other, "I expect you will keep your word"; to you, I reply: "You can count on me"' (1992: 286).
2. Solicitude: respecting others and their uniqueness as I respect myself. Viewing other people as irreplaceable and caring about them. This is not just friendship, but recognizing the suffering of others.
3. Self-esteem: which is the wish to live a good life, to esteem ourselves and others. This is the aim of an ethical life.
4. Reciprocity: where one hears and responds to others. Reciprocity involves dignity and respecting others for who they are.
5. Living well with others: which involves both interpersonal relations and justice and equality within institutions.

And, as you may see, ethical selfhood is different from idem identity because it's not about how we are the same as others, but about how we are the same over time (self-constant and true to our word) and how we respect our differences with others. So we experience the possibilities of who we are in relational moments of solicitude, reciprocity and self-constancy. In practical terms this involves establishing relationships of mutual respect, appreciation and in creating good energy to work together.

Ethical selfhood is not about managing or manipulating relationships, neither is it about blaming the situation as being at fault, it *is* about recognizing that we have a moral and social responsibility to understand what we can, and should, expect of ourselves and others. Ricoeur believes we have a personal responsibility for ethical action and, because we are always in-relation to others, we have a duty of care to them.

Thus, it's important for managers to consider *how* they relate to others; what assumptions they hold about people; to understand how others may view the world; to be open to those different views; and to create opportunities for open dialogue. This is an interpersonal ethics of managing, based on understanding who I am as a manager. It's a relational ethics which places responsibility for ethical ways of being and ethical action on myself. *Who I am in relation to others is important!*

### Managing just and moral institutions

Ricoeur's work also connects with ethics and managing moral organizations because he is concerned with what just institutions might look like. Whereas ethics is about aiming for the good life, morality is about moral norms and justice, and justice is about equality and what is legal. He rejects a foundational or universal view of ethics – the Kantian idea of objective and universal moral laws, saying that ethics is 'enriched by the passage through the norm and exercising moral judgment in a given situation' (Ricoeur, 1992: 203). In other words, we need moral norms, but both they, and we as moral agents, are situated within a history and a social context that should not be ignored.

Ricoeur also argues that conflict is unavoidable in moral life because of 'the agonistic ground of human experience' (1992: 243); the differences that exist between old and young, society and individuals, male and female, and so on. Conflict also occurs within institutions because of different views about what is a 'just distribution' of goods, responsibilities, rights, etc.; different views about what is good government, and over how government or, more specifically, democracy is legitimized. You can perhaps begin to see the links with managing organizations. Ricoeur's work asks us to recognize that organizations are a play of voices, connected by a bond of common practices and customs rather than rules, in which each individual has a responsibility to herself or himself, as well as to other organizational members, to act in ethical and moral ways. Ricoeur doesn't ignore the dark side – he acknowledges that evil exists and that we do violence to each other in various intended and unintended ways. But he calls on us to recognize our responsibility *not* to do violence to others.

Violence might seem like a strong word to use, for it implies aggression, bullying, sexual harassment and verbal abuse, all of which occur in organizations. But violence can also take more insidious forms. Marie-France Hirigoyen (2005) talks about *moral harassment* – emotional violence caused by behaviour, words, facial expressions and gestures that degrade others. Neglect, ignoring employees by not giving them training or work assignment opportunities are examples of forms of violence. Inaction can also be a form of violence in the sense that not acting against such behaviours can be seen as a form of complicity.

Stephen Linstead addresses this issue in discussing *organizational bystanding*, 'where we know and may even witness the sort of injustice or bullying entailed by moral harassment, but do nothing about it' (2006: 208). He argues this can take three forms: ignoring what's happening around us; seeing injustice or moral harassment but failing to recognize it as such; or recognizing injustice or moral harassment and refusing to act, for whatever reason. I have experienced the latter – imagine working in a department culture where bullying and unequal treatment of employees is well-known, and yet no one is willing to inform senior managers in the organization for fear of reprisal. Peter Verhezen (2010) argues that a culture of moral silence in an organization is not just about not whistleblowing, but is also about not questioning or speaking up against morally suspect policies, decisions and actions – and not speaking out for morally valued actions and relationships. Ethical and open dialogue, along with ethical narratives, can help support a culture of integrity. So dialogue is not around, 'What can we legally get away with?' but 'What is the right, morally excellent, thing to do?'

For Ricoeur, solicitude is crucial at the interpersonal and the institutional level. In the latter he defines solicitude as a concern for others through justice. To encapsulate his complex discussion of morality, he argues that just institutions are about the exercise of moral judgement and about *taking part* or deliberating well (1992: 247), which is tied in with power. Ricoeur talks about three forms of power:

- *Power over* is a form of violence exerted over others, including deceit (self-deceit and deceiving others), manipulation, domination and physical violence, which destroy respect and lead to suffering. Hierarchical organizations embody this form of power in many ways, not just in terms of managerial authority, but through the more insidious forms of power we discussed in Chapter 4.
- *Power-to-do* is the power to act and to be able to see myself as the author of my action. This isn't formal power as we typically think about it, but knowing that I can shape my experience and myself in

my everyday actions and interactions – in other words managers as practical authors and reflexive practitioners.

- *Power-in-common* is the ability of people to live together well in a community, the power of plurality: recognizing that conflicts are inherent to institutional life, are open and negotiable, and can lead to new ways of living together. It's within this sense of power-in-common that our commitment and our ability to deliberate well are crucial – to recognize and respect others and work together to imagine what new forms of life or organization might look like.

There have been a number of scholarly criticisms of Ricoeur's work that may be read at leisure. I'd like to end this chapter by looking at how we can take his work into the context of managing organizations: how it might offer a different lens on ethical management.

Ricoeur places ethics as a moral and relational activity, around the fundamental challenge to *live well with others in just institutions*. This seems like an ideal we can extend to our organizational lives. In doing so, it's important to have ethical codes of conduct because they establish the moral norms against which we can evaluate ethical action. But what is crucially important to ethical organizational practice, to managing organizations in ethical ways, is the ethical intention and action of individual organizational members. Ethics is about relationality – *who we are and how we relate to others* – and this becomes particularly important in asymmetrical relationships – where one person has power over another. This means being self-reflexive about who I am as a person and as a manager, questioning my assumptions and actions, recognizing that I am responsible for what I do and say, while also being responsible for others, because I cannot separate myself from others, in both a particular and a general sense. Managers also need to be critically-reflexive about organizational culture, policies and practices … so that they do not, in Ricoeur's terms, do violence to others.

I began this chapter by saying that I'm a moral optimist – I think it's a prerequisite to living your life in this way. As Chris Grey says at the end of the very first *Very Short …* book: 'The stakes are very high. What kind of a world do you want?'

### And so …?

So let's assume we want to manage ethically – and by this I mean in responsive and responsible ways – what might we do? Well, we need to begin by recognizing that we are no longer well served by many forms of current management and organizational practices; that there are possibilities for new forms of ethical practice that we can success-fully build with organizational members; and that central to this is our own sense of who we are and how we relate to others.

Merleau-Ponty (1964: 109) argues that if we understand ourselves as in-relation to others, a new idea of truth emerges, one that lies in rela-tionships not in the situation. In other words, we cannot blame the situation as being at fault because we have a moral and social respon-sibility to understand what we can (and should) expect of ourselves and others (Cunliffe, 2009: 95).

I want to give the last word to one of my students, who really cap-tured in a very practical way the implications of Ricoeur's ideas on ethical selfhood for managers. He ended his paper by saying:[7]

First, I want to work more closely with other effective leaders who apply reflexive or highly ethical approaches to their work (e.g. Duffy Swan or Don Chalmers). Often these types of leaders operate quietly but effectively and I will need to search for them in unexpected places. As I learned from a classmate, Don Chalmers quietly volunteers his time at the Road Runner Food Bank. I plan to spend more of my time providing volunteer ser-vices now too. Rich Marquez listed many attributes of successful leaders. I hope to focus more on those attributes I am weakest in such as humility for self and empathy with others. I also intend to search for non-traditional leaders such as those who provide services to me and my organization.

Second, I am personally committed to reading and learning more about the philosophies of leadership espoused by Chatterjee (1998) and other 'non-traditional' or non-western leadership writ-ers. My exposure to and understanding of leadership philosophies in other cultures is too limited. I work with others from different cultures and I hope to better understand and appreciate our mutual values and differences. I am seriously considering taking educational classes in meditation and eastern philosophies and participating in cultural events to help me to better understand and apply cultural norms that differ from my own.

Finally, the most important element of my personal growth plan will be my ability to encourage an enduring generative learning approach to life and a critically reflexive view of my own actions. Finding a mentor may be especially helpful for achieving this goal. As Sheri Milone pointed out, developing a relationship with a mentor can be most beneficial for becoming a more aware and effective leader. I will need to search for such a mentor as there are many effective leaders in my organization. However I do not expect to easily find someone with the skills and philosophies I hope to nourish. Until I am successful at finding such a willing mentor I intend to develop a personal mental checklist or mindset that operates intuitively to help me be a more reflexive thinker. I also intend to develop a feedback or performance monitoring behavior (Drucker, 1999) that warns me when I have strayed. However, I must rely for now on my own mental discipline to develop and stay true to this leadership growth strategy. It will be a challenge but I expect to meet it. I will be an effective Philosopher Leader!

## Notes

1. See http://group.barclays.com/about-barclays/citizenship/policy-positions (accessed 20 July 2013).
2. See Armenakis (2002) for an interview with Morton-Thiokol engineer Roger Boisjoly on ethics and the story. See also: www.nasaspaceflight.com/2007/01/remembering-the-mistakes-of-challenger/ (accessed 4 September 2013).
3. You can view a range of their adverts at www.visit4ads.com/brand/The-Co-operative-Bank/6867 (accessed 4 September 2013).
4. http://m1.ethisphere.com/wme2013/index.html (accessed 10 September 2013).
5. Based on a personal communication from Normi Noel (1995), cited in Gilligan (1995: 121).
6. www.youtube.com/watch?v=TDjxDL00mvg (accessed 22 July 2013).
7. Quoted with permission.

# Conclusion

In writing the conclusion to the book, I ended up with a long version and a short version – a bit like writing two different endings to a story. The long version summarized and explained the key themes, based on the golden rule of 'Telling the reader what you said'. But we've dealt with some challenging ideas about management and I wanted to capture the nub. The short version (the one here) is the pithy story, which, if you've already read the book, will mean you'll look at the key issues and hopefully say 'yep', 'got that', 'makes sense', and 'at last, it all falls into place!'...

And if you are one of those people who like to know the ending before you read the story, then these snippets will hopefully intrigue you enough to want to read more.

So here goes:

This book offers a different 'critical' lens for viewing management, managers and managing organizations – it's not a book about management techniques.

The main theme of the book is that managing is a relational, reflexive and ethical activity. It is not just something one *does*, but is more crucially *who one is* and *how we relate to others*.

Managers and organizations play a pivotal role in the world today, because what they do has an impact on everyone's lives.

Despite 100 years of management theories and techniques, managing is still difficult – most of us have experienced working for ineffective managers or had a bad experience as a customer.

Why is managing so difficult? Because managers are like the rest of us – human and fallible.

People interpret the world and themselves differently; we have our own ideas about what's important and what needs to be done, and we like to do things our own way. We are naturally inquisitive, suspicious, we love, laugh, get scared and dislike others. This doesn't stop the moment we walk into work. And what's rational to me is not necessarily rational to you – so, why should I buy into your version of rationality?

So, what if we question taken-for-granted views about management, and explore some different ways of thinking about management and managers?

Life in organizations is messy, complex, open to various interpretations and therefore contestable – it's not predictable and controllable, people engage in overt and subtle acts of resistance.

This surely means that the more ways managers have of viewing the world and of exploring possibilities, the better able they will be to manage in responsive, responsible and ethical ways.

Managing is about somehow connecting with people, recognizing and respecting differences and creating meaning. Managing is relational and reflexive.

This means that instead of taking a realist view of the world as existing outside us, we assume that we have a dialectical relationship with our social world – we shape and are shaped by our experience as we talk and interact with others. We socially construct our world.

Language is therefore important, because we shape meaning, understanding and actions in relationally-responsive interactions and conversations with others. But language is not precise – it works in subtle ways. We need to be aware how.

Managing relationally is about dialogue not monologue, seeing conversations as crucial ways of figuring out between us what needs to be done.

Managers are always engaged in identity-work – shaping their sense of who they are in relation to others.

We can use these ideas about social reality and language to both *understand* management and *be* managers differently. So, what might we see if we look at organizational culture, power and responsibility within relationships of difference? How might this influence the way we manage people and organizations? Can managers become cultural explorers and adventurers rather than manipulators?

Is culture a 'cult'?

Organizational culture emerges continually in our actions, conversations, texts and symbols, and is open to many interpretations and reinterpretations. Organizational culture also privileges particular ideologies and groups and marginalizes other.

And managers should be ethical – but we are still rocked by corporate scandals. Why? Does it have something to do with the focus on efficiency and on management techniques as value-neutral activities?

What if ethical management is both relational *and* institutional? About how we treat people and live our lives with others as well as moral codes of practice?

Being ethical means understanding who we are in relation to others and recognizing that we have a moral and social responsibility to understand what we can and should expect of ourselves and others.

Being a manager is inseparable from who we are and how we relate to others, which means being *care*ful and thoughtful in what we say and do.

Which brings us back to managing as relational, reflexive and ethical ....

# References

Acker, J. (2005) *Class Questions, Feminist Answers*. Lanham, MD: Rowman & Littlefield.

Adams, G.P. (1911) 'Beyond moral idealism', *Harvard Theological Review*, 4 (2): 229–40.

Agar, M. (1994) *Language Shock: Understanding the Culture of Conversation*. New York: Perennial.

Alvesson, M. and Deetz, S. (2000) *Doing Critical Management Research*. London: Sage.

Alvesson, M. and Willmott, H. (eds) (1992) *Critical Management Studies*. London: Sage.

Alvesson, M. and Willmott, H. (1996) *Making Sense of Management: A Critical Introduction*. London: Sage.

Argyris, C. (1982) *Reasoning, Learning and Action: Individual and Organizational*. San Francisco: Jossey Bass.

Argyris, C. (1991) 'Teaching smart people how to learn', *Harvard Business Review*, 69 (3): 99–110.

Argyris, C. and Schön, D. (1974) *Theory in Practice: Increasing Professional Effectiveness*. San Francisco: Jossey Bass.

Armenakis, A.A. (2002) 'Boisjoly on ethics: an interview with Roger Boisjoly', *Journal of Management Inquiry*, 11 (3): 274–81.

Ashcraft. K.L. (2001a) 'Organized dissonance: feminist bureaucracy as hybrid form', *Academy of Management Journal*, 44 (6): 1301–22.

Ashcraft. K.L. (2001b) 'Feminist organizing and the construction of "alternative" community', in J.G. Shepherd and E.W. Rothenbuhler (eds), *Communication and Community*. Mahwah, NJ: LEA Publishers, pp. 79–110.

Ashcraft, K.L. and Mumby, D. (2004) *Reworking Gender: A Feminist Communicology of Organization*. Thousand Oaks, CA: Sage.

Austin, J.L. (1962) *How to Do Things With Words*. Cambridge, MA: Harvard University Press.

Bakhtin, M.M. (1981) *The Dialogical Imagination: Four Essays by M.M. Bakhtin*, ed. M. Holquist, trans. C. Emerson and M. Holquist. Austin: University of Texas Press [reprinted 2002].

Bakhtin, M.M. (1984) *Problems of Dostoevsky's Poetics*. Manchester: Manchester University Press.

Bakhtin, M.M. (1986) *Speech Genres and Other Late Essays*, trans. V.W. McGee. Austin: University of Texas Press [reprinted 1996].

Banerjee, S.B. and Tedmanson, D. (2010) 'Grass burning under our feet: indigenous enterprise development in a political economy of whiteness', *Management Learning*, 41 (2): 147–65.

Barker, R. (2010) 'Management in *not* a profession', *Harvard Business Review*, 88 (7/8): 52–60.

Barnard, C. (1938) *The Functions of the Executive*. Cambridge, MA: Harvard University Press.

Baudrillard, J. (1994) *Simulacra and Simulations*, trans. S. F. Glaser. Ann Arbor: The University of Michigan Press.

Bentham, J. (1789) *An Introduction to the Principles of Morals and Legislation*.

Berger, P.L. and Luckmann, T. (1966) *The Social Construction of Reality: A Treatise in the Sociology of Knowledge*. New York: Anchor Books, Doubleday.

Bhabha, H.K. (1994) *The Location of Culture*. London: Routledge.

Biehl-Missal, B (2011) 'Business is show business: management presentations as performance', *Journal of Management Studies*, 48 (3): 619–45.

Boje, D.M. (1991) 'The storytelling organization: a study of story performance in an office-supply firm', *Administrative Science Quarterly*, 36 (1): 106–26.

Boje, D.M. (2008) *Storytelling Organizations*. London: Sage.

Borofsky, R. (2005) *Yanomami: The Fierce Controversy and What We Can Learn from it*. Berkeley, CA: University of California Press.

Boyatzis, R.E. (1982) *The Competent Manager: A Model for Effective Performance*. New York: John Wiley & Sons.

Braverman, H. (1974) *Labor and Monopoly Capital: The Degradation of Work in the Twentieth Century*. New York: Monthly Review Press.

Brewis, J. (1999) 'How does it feel? Women managers, embodiment and changing public sector cultures', in S. Whitehead and R. Moodley (eds), *Transforming Managers: Gendering Change in the Public Sector*. London: UCL Press, pp. 84–106.

Brown, A.D. and Humphreys, M. (2006) 'Organizational identity and place: a discursive exploration of hegemony and resistance', *Journal of Management Studies*, 43 (2): 231–57.

Butler, J. (1990) *Gender Trouble: Feminism and the Subversion of Identity*. New York: Routledge [reprinted 1999].

Butler, J. (1993) *Bodies That Matter: On the Discursive Limits of Sex*. London: Routledge.

Carlson, S. (1951) *Executive Behaviour*. Stockholm: Strömbergs.

Carter, C., Clegg, S.R. and Kornberger, M. (2008) *A Very Short, Fairly Interesting and Reasonably Cheap Book about Studying Strategy*. London: Sage.

Centre for Women and Democracy (2013) *Sex and Power 2013: Who Runs Britain?* Available at: www.countingwomenin.org/wp-content/uploads/2013/02/Sex-and-Power-2013-FINALv2.-pdf.pdf (accessed 13 July 2013).

Chapman, M.R. (2006) *In Search of Stupidity: Over 20 Years of High-Tech Marketing Disasters* (2nd edn). Berkley, CA: Apress.

Chatterjee, D. (1998) *Leading Consciously: A Pilgrimage Toward Self-Mastery.* Boston, MA: Butterworth Heinemann.

Chia, R. and Morgan, S. (1996) 'Educating the philosopher manager, designing the times', *Management Learning*, 27 (1): 37–64.

Clifford, J. (1983) 'On ethnographic authority', *Representations*, 1 (2): 118–46.

Collins, D. (2012) 'Women roar: "The women's thing" in the storywork of Tom Peters', *Organization*, 19 (4): 405–24.

Contu, A. (2008) 'Decaf resistance: on misbehavior, cynicism, and desire in liberal workplaces', *Management Communication Quarterly*, 21 (3): 364–79.

Cunliffe, A.L. (2001) 'Managers as practical authors: reconstructing our understanding of management practice', *Journal of Management Studies*, 38 (3): 351–71.

Cunliffe, A.L. (2002a) 'Social poetics: a dialogical approach to management inquiry', *Journal of Management Inquiry*, 11 (2): 128–46.

Cunliffe, A.L. (2002b) 'Reflexive dialogical practice in management learning', *Management Learning*, 33 (1): 35–61.

Cunliffe, A.L. (2008) 'Orientations to social constructionism: relationally-responsive social constructionism and its implications for knowledge and learning', *Management Learning*, 39 (2): 123–39.

Cunliffe, A.L. (2009) 'The philosopher leader: on relationalism, ethics and reflexivity – a critical perspective on teaching leadership', *Management Learning*, 40 (1): 87–101.

Cunliffe A.L. and Eriksen, M. (2011) 'Relational leadership', *Human Relations*, 64 (11): 1425–49.

Currie, D., McElwee, G. and Somerville, P. (2012) 'Managerialism and nihilism', *Tamara, Journal of Critical Postmodern Organization Science*, 10 (4): 61–72.

Deal, T. and Kennedy, A. (1982) *Corporate Cultures: The Rites and Rituals of Corporate Life.* Reading, MA: Addison-Wesley.

Deem, R. and Brehony, K.J. (2005) 'Management as ideology: the case of "new managerialism" in higher education', *Oxford Review of Education*, 31 (2): 217–35.

Deetz, S.A. (1992) *Democracy in an Age of Corporate Colonization: Developments in Communication and the Politics of Everyday Life.* Albany: State University of New York Press.

Derrida, J. (1978) *Writing and Différance.* London: Routledge & Kegan Paul.

Dewey, J. (1910) *How We Think.* Mineola, NY: Dover Publications, Inc. [reprinted 1997].

Drucker, P.F. (1973) *Management: Tasks, Responsibilities, Practices*. New York: Harper & Row.

Drucker, P. (1999) 'Managing oneself', *Harvard Business Review*, March, 77 (2): 65–74.

Eisenstein, H. (1996) *Inside Agitators: Australian Femocrats and the State*. Philadelphia, PA: Temple University Press.

EOWA (2006) *Australian Census of Women in Leadership*. Available at www.wgea.gov.au/sites/default/files/2006__EOWA_Census_Publication_tagged.pdf (accessed 4 September 2013).

Escobar, A. (1995) *Encountering Development: The Making and Unmaking of the Third World*. Princeton, NJ: Princeton University Press.

Fairclough, N. (2003) *Analysing Discourse, Textual Analysis for Social Research*. London: Routledge.

Fairhurst, G. and Sarr, R. (1996) *The Art of Framing*. San Francisco: Jossey-Bass.

Fayol, H. (1949) *General and Industrial Management*. London: Pitman [first published 1916].

Fine, M., Weis, L. and Powell, L.C. (1997) 'Communities of difference: a critical look at desegregated spaces created for and by youth', *Harvard Educational Review*, 67 (2): 247–84.

Fineman, S. (2011) *Organizing Age*. Oxford: Oxford University Press.

Fleming, P. and Sturdy, A. (2011) '"Being yourself" in the electronic sweatshop: new forms of normative control', *Human Relations*, 64 (2): 177–200.

Fletcher, J. (1998) 'Relational practice: a feminist reconstruction of work', *Journal of Management Inquiry*, 7 (2): 163–88.

Follett, M.P. (1918) *The New State: Group Organization and the Solution of Popular Government*. New York: Longman, Green & Co.

Follett, M.P. (1924) *Creative Experience*. New York: Longman, Green & Co.

Ford, J. (2006) 'Discourses of leadership, gender, identity and contradiction in a UK public sector organization', *Leadership*, 2 (1): 77–99.

Ford, J. and Harding, N. (2007) 'Move over management, we are all leaders now', *Management Learning*, 38 (5): 1350–76.

Ford, J.D., Ford, L.W. and McNamara, R.T. (2002) 'Resistance and the background conversations of change', *Journal of Organizational Change Management*, 15 (2): 105–21.

Foucault, M. (1970) *The Order of Things: An Archaeology of the Human Sciences*. London: Routledge.

Foucault, M. (1972) *The Archaeology of Knowledge*, trans. A.M. Sheridan Smith. New York: Pantheon Books.

Foucault, M. (1980) *The History of Sexuality, Vol. 1: An Introduction*. New York: Vintage Books.

Foucault, M. (1988) *The Care of the Self: The History of Sexuality*. New York: Vintage Books.

French, R. and Grey, C. (eds) (1996) *Rethinking Management Education*. London: Sage.

Gabriel, Y. (1995) 'The unmanaged organization: stories, fantasies and subjectivity', *Organization Studies*, 16 (3): 477–501.

Gabriel, Y. and Connell, N.A.D. (2010) 'Co-creating stories: collaborative experiments in storytelling', *Management Learning*, 41 (5): 507–23.

Garfinkel, H. (1967) *Studies in Ethnomethodology*. Englewood Cliffs, NJ: Prentice Hall.

Geertz, C. (1983) *Local Knowledge*. New York: Basic Books.

Gherardi, S. (1995) *Gender, Symbolism and Organizational Cultures*. London: Sage.

Gherardi, S. (2009) 'Introduction: the critical power of the "practice lens"', *Management Learning*, 40 (2): 115–28.

Ghoshal, S. (2005) 'Bad management theories are destroying good management practices', *Academy of Management Learning and Education*, 4 (1): 75–91.

Gilligan, C. (1982) *In a Different Voice: Psychological Theory and Women's Development*. Cambridge, MA: Harvard University Press.

Gilligan, C. (1995) 'Hearing the difference: theorizing connection', *Hypatia*, 10 (2): 120–27.

Goffman, E. (1959) *The Presentation of Self in Everyday Life*. London: Allen Lane.

Goffman, E. (1961) *Asylums*. Harmondsworth: Penguin [reprinted 1976].

Goffman, E. (1967) *Interaction Ritual: Essays on Face-to-face Behavior*. New York: Random House Inc.

Gowler, D. and Legge, K. (1996) 'The meaning of management and the management of meaning', in S. Linstead, R. Grafton Small and P. Jeffcutt (eds), *Understanding Management*. London: Sage, pp. 34–50.

Gramsci, A. (1971) *Selections from the Prison Notebooks*, trans. Q. Hoare and G. Nowell-Smith. New York: International.

Greener, I. (2007) 'The politics of gender in the NHS: impression management and "getting things done"', *Gender, Work and Organization*, 14 (3): 281–99.

Grey, C. (2013) *A Very Short, Fairly Interesting and Reasonably Cheap Book about Studying Organizations*. London: Sage [first published 2006].

Grey, C. and Willmott, H. (eds) (2005) *Critical Management Studies: A Reader*. Oxford: Oxford University Press.

Gulick, L. and Urwick, L. (eds) (1937) *Papers on the Science of Administration*. New York: Institute of Public Administration, Columbia University.

Hales, C.P. (1986) 'What do managers do? A critical review', *Journal of Management Studies*, 23 (1): 88–115.

Harding, N. (2003) *The Social Construction of Management: Texts and Identities*. London: Routledge.

Hatch, M.J. (1997) 'Irony and the social construction of contradiction in the humor of a management team', *Organization Science*, 8 (3): 275–88.

Hatch, M.J. with Cunliffe, A.L. (2013) *Organization Theory: Modern, Symbolic, and Postmodern Perspectives* (3rd edn). Oxford: Oxford University Press.

Hay Group (2001) *The Manager Competency Model*. Available at: www.professional-learning.com/MCPBriefGuide.pdf (accessed 4 September 2013).

Haynes, K (2012) 'Body beautiful? Gender, identity and the body in professional services firms', *Gender, Work and Organization*, 19 (5): 399–507.

Heidegger, M. (1966) *Discourse on Thinking: A Translation of Gelassenheit*, trans. J.M. Anderson and E. Hans Freund. New York: Harper & Row.

Henderson, B.B.J. (2002) *A Conflict of Interest: Fraud and the Collapse of Titans*. Lincoln, NE: Writers Club Press.

Heusinkveld, S., Sturdy, A. and Werr, A. (2011) 'The co-consumption of management ideas and practices', *Management Learning*, 42 (2): 139–47.

Highhouse, S., Brooks, M.E. and Gregarus, G. (2009) 'An organizational impression management perspective on the formation of corporate reputations', *Journal of Management*, 35 (6): 1481–93.

Hirigoyen, M.-F. (2005) *Stalking the Soul: Emotional Abuse and the Erosion of Identity*, trans. H. Marx and T. Moore. New York: Helen Marx Books.

Hobbes, T. (1651) *Leviathan: The Matter, Forme and Power of a Commonwealth Ecclesiastical and Civil*.

Hochschild, A.R. (1983) *The Managed Heart: Commercialization of Human Feeling*. Berkeley: University of California Press.

Hofstede, G. (1985) 'The interaction between national and organizational value systems', *Journal of Management Studies*, 22 (4): 347–57.

Hofstede, G. (2001) *Culture's Consequences: Comparing Values, Behaviors, Institutions and Organizations* (2nd edn). Thousand Oaks, CA: Sage.

Hood, C.C. and Jackson, M.W. (1991) *Administrative Argument*. Aldershot: Dartmouth

Höpfl, H. (2002) 'Playing the part: reflections on aspects of mere performance in the customer–client relationship', *Journal of Management Studies*, 39 (2): 255–67.

Horne, J.H. and Lupton, T. (1965) 'The work activities of "middle managers": an exploratory study', *Journal of Management Studies*, 2 (1): 14–33.

Husserl, E. (1983) *Ideas Pertaining to a Pure Phenomenology and to a Phenomenological Philosophy*. First Book, trans. F. Kersten. Netherlands: Kluwer Academic Publishers [reprinted 1998].

Jack, G., Westwood, R., Srinivas, N. and Sardar, Z. (2011) 'Deepening, broadening and re-asserting a postcolonial interrogative space in organization studies', *Organization*, 18 (3): 275–302.

Jackall, R. (1988) *Moral Mazes: The World of Corporate Managers*. New York: Oxford University Press.

Jassawalla, A.R. and Sashittal, H.C. (2002) 'Cultures that support product innovation processes', *Academy of Management Executive*, 16 (3): 42–54.

Kahney, L. (2008) 'How Apple got everything right by doing everything wrong', *Wired Magazine*. Available at www.wired.com/techbiz/it/magazine/16-04/bz_apple?currentPage=all (accessed 11 July 2013).

Kakabadse, A., Bank, J. and Vinnicombe, S. (2004) *Working in Organizations* (2nd edn). Aldershot: Gower Publishing.

Kalonaityte, V. (2010) 'The case of vanishing borders: theorizing diversity management as internal border control', *Organization*, 17 (1): 31–52.

Kant, I. (1785) *Fundamental Principles of the Metaphysic of Morals*.

Kantola, A. and Seeck, H. (2011) 'Dissemination of management into politics: Michael Porter and the political uses of management consulting', *Management Learning*, 42 (1): 25–47.

Keenoy, T. and Seijo, G. (2009) 'Re-imagining e-mail: academics in the castle', *Organization*, 17 (2): 177–98.

Kelan, E.R. (2013) 'The becoming of business bodies: gender, appearance, and leadership development', *Management Learning*, 44 (1): 45–61.

Kenny, C. and Fraser, T.N. (2012) *Living Indigenous Leadership: Native Narratives on Building Strong Communities*. Vancouver: University of British Columbia Press.

Kepner, C.H. and Tregoe, B.B. (1965) *The Rational Manager: A Systematic Approach to Problem Solving and Decision Making*. New York: McGraw Hill.

Khurana, R. (2007) *From Higher Aims to Hired Hands: The Social Transformation of American Business Schools and the Unfulfilled Promise of Management as a Profession*. Princeton, NJ: Princeton University Press.

Kirkpatrick, G. (2009) *The Corporate Governance Lessons from the Financial Crisis*, OECD Report. Available at: www.oecd.org/finance/financial-markets/42229620.pdf (accessed 4 September 2013).

Kohlberg, L. (1969) 'Stage and sequence: the cognitive-developmental approach to socialization', in D.A. Goslin (ed.), *Handbook of Socialization Theory and Research*. Chicago: Rand McNally, pp. 347–480.

Koning, J. and Waistell, J. (2012) 'Identity talk of aspirational ethical leaders', *Journal of Business Ethics*, 107 (1): 65–77.

Korczynski, M. (2011) 'The dialectical sense of humour: routine joking in a Taylorized factory', *Organization Studies*, 32 (10): 1421–39.

Kornberger, M., Justesen, L. and Mouritsen, J. (2011) 'When you make manager we put a big mountain in front of you: an ethnography of managers in a big 4 accounting firm', *Accounting, Organizations and Society*, 36 (8): 514–33.

Kotter, J.P. (1977) 'Power, dependence, and effective management', *Harvard Business Review*, 55 (4): 125–36.

Kotter, J.P. (1982) *The General Managers*. New York: Free Press.

Kunda, G. (1992) *Engineering Culture*. Philadelphia, PA: Temple University Press.

Laclau E. and Mouffe, C. (1985) *Hegemony and Socialist Strategy: Towards a Radical Democratic Politics*. London: Verso.

Lawler, E.E. (ed.) (1985) *Doing Research That Is Useful in Theory and Practice*. San Francisco: Jossey Bass.

Learmonth, M. and Harding, N. (2006) 'Evidence-based management, the very idea', *Public Administration*, 84 (2): 245–66.

Lewin, S. and Reeves, S. (2011) 'Enacting "team" and "teamwork": using Goffman's theory of impression management to illuminate interprofessional practice in hospital wards', *Social Science and Medicine*, 72 (10): 1595–602.

Linstead, S. (2006) 'The comedy of ethics: the New York four, the duty of care and organizational bystanding', in R. Westwood and C. Rhodes (eds), *Humour, Work and Organization*. London: Routledge, pp. 203–31.

Liu, H. (2010) 'When leaders fail: a typology of failures and framing strategies', *Management Communication Quarterly*, 24 (2): 232–59.

Luhman, J.T. and Cunliffe, A.L. (2012) *Key Concepts in Organization Theory*. London: Sage.

Lukes, S. (1974) *Power: A Radical View*. London: Macmillan.

MacIntyre, A. (2007) *After Virtue: A Study in Moral Theory* (3rd edn). Notre Dame, IN: University of Notre Dame Press [first published 1981].

*Management Learning* (2009) Special Issue: Teaching from Critical Perspectives, 40 (1).

Marcus, G.E. and Fischer, M. (1986) *Anthropology as Cultural Critique*. Chicago: University of Chicago Press.

Martin, J. (1990) 'Deconstructing organizational taboos: the suppression of gender conflict in organizations', *Organization Science*, 1 (4): 339–59.

Maslow, A.H. (1943) 'A theory of human motivation', *Psychological Review*, 50 (4): 370–96.

McCabe, D. (2008) 'Who's afraid of enterprise? Producing and repressing the enterprise self in a UK bank', *Organization*, 15 (3): 371–87.

Medvedev, P.N. and Bakhtin, M.M. (1978) *The Formal Method in Literary Scholarship: A Critical Introduction to Sociological Poetics*, trans. A.J. Wehrle. Baltimore, MD: John Hopkins University Press.

Merleau-Ponty, M. (1962) *Phenomenology of Perception*, trans. C. Smith. London and New York: Routledge [reprinted 2004].

Merleau-Ponty, M. (1964) *Signs*, trans. R.C. McCleary. Evanston, IL: Northwestern University Press.

Mill, J.S. (1861) *Representative Government*.

Mintzberg, H. (1973) *The Nature of Managerial Work*. New York: Harper & Row.

Morgan, G. (1986) *Images of Organization*. London: Sage [reprinted 2006].

Mumby, D.K. (2005) 'Theorizing resistance in organization studies: a dialectical approach', *Management Communication Quarterly*, 19 (1): 19–44.

Nicolini, D. (2011) 'Practice as the site of knowing: insights from the field of telemedicine', *Organization Science*, 22 (3): 602–20.

Nkomo, S.M. (2011) 'A postcolonial and anti-colonial reading of "African" leadership and management in organization studies: tensions, contradictions and possibilities', *Organization*, 18 (3): 365–86.

Orr, K. and Bennett, M. (2012) 'Public administration scholarship and the politics of coproducing academic–practitioner research', *Public Administration Review*, 72 (4): 487–95.

Ortiz, S.J. (2002) 'Culture and the universe', in *Out There Somewhere*. Tuscon, AZ: University of Arizona Press, pp. 104–5.

Owen, D. (2012) *The Hubris Syndrome: Bush, Blair and the Intoxication of Power* (2nd edn). York: Methuen.

Özkazanç-Pan, B. (2008) 'International management research meets "the rest of the world"', *Academy of Management Review*, 33 (4): 964–74.

Palmer, I. and Hardy, C. (2000) *Thinking about Management: Implications of Organizational Debates for Practice*. London: Sage.

Parker, M. (ed.) (1998) *Ethics and Organizations*. London: Sage.

Parker, M. (2002) *Against Management: Organization in the Age of Materialism*. Cambridge: Polity Press.

Peters, T.J. and Waterman, R.H. (1982) *In Search of Excellence: Lessons from America's Best Run Companies*. New York: Harper & Row.

Petit, V. and Bollaert, H. (2012) 'Flying too close to the sun? Hubris among CEOs and how to prevent it', *Journal of Business Ethics*, 108 (3): 265–83.

Pfeffer, J. (1992) *Managing with Power*. Cambridge, MA: Harvard Business School Press.

Pfeffer, J. and Fong, C.T. (2002) 'The end of business schools? Less success than meets the eye', *Academy of Management Learning and Education*, 1 (1): 78–95.

Pfeffer, J. and Sutton, R.I. (2006) 'Evidence-based management', *Harvard Business Review*, 84 (1): 62–74.

Phillips, M. and Knowles, D. (2012) 'Performance and performativity: undoing fictions of women business owner', *Gender, Work and Organization*, 19 (4): 416–37.

Poff, D.C. (2010) 'Ethical leadership and global citizenship: considerations for a just and sustainable future', *Journal of Business Ethics*, 93 (1): 9–14.

Powell, W.W. and DiMaggio, P.J. (1983) (eds) *The New Institutionalism in Organizational Analysis*. Chicago: University of Chicago Press.

Prasad, A. and Prasad, P. (2001) '(Un)willing to resist? The discursive production of local workplace opposition', *Studies in Culture, Organizations and Societies*, 7 (1): 105–25.

Prusak, L., Groh, K., Denning, S. and Seely Brown, J. (2011) *Storytelling in Organizations: Why Storytelling Is Transforming 21st Century Organizations and Management*. Oxford: Elsevier, Butterworth Heinemann.

Pullen, A. (2006) *Managing Identity*. Basingstoke: Palgrave Macmillan.

Rawls, J. (1971) *A Theory of Justice*. Cambridge, MA: Belknap Press of Harvard University Press.

Reedy, P. (2009) *The Manager's Tale: Stories of Managerial Identity*. Farnham: Ashgate Publishing.

Rice, J.H. (1960) 'Existentialism for the businessman', *Harvard Business Review*, 38 (2): 135–43.

Ricoeur, P. (1992) *Oneself as Another*, trans. K. Blamey. Chicago: University of Chicago Press.

Ritzer, G. (1995) *The McDonaldization of Society: An Investigation into the Changing Character of Contemporary Social Life*. Thousand Oaks: Pine Forge Press.

Said, E.W. (1993) *Culture and Imperialism*. New York: Knopf.

Salancik, G.R. and Pfeffer, J. (1977) 'Who gets power – and how they hold on to it: a strategic contingency model of power', *Organizational Dynamics*, 5 (3): 3–21.

Sandberg, S. with Scovell, N. (2013) *Lean In: Women, Work and the Will to Lead*. New York: Alfred A Knopf.

Sartre, J.-P. (1956) *Being and Nothingness: A Phenomenological Essay on Ontology*. New York: Citadel Press, Kensington Publishing [reprinted 2001].

Saussure, F. de (1959). *Course in General Linguistics*, trans. Wade Baskin. New York: McGraw-Hill [first published 1911].

Sayles, L.R. (1964) *Managerial Behavior.* New York: McGraw-Hill.

Schein, E.H. (1985) *Organizational Culture and Leadership* (2nd edn). San Francisco: Jossey-Bass.

Schön, D.A. (1983) *The Reflective Practitioner: How Professionals Think in Action.* New York: Basic Books.

Shamir, B. (2007) 'Strategic leadership as management of meanings', in R. Hooijberg, J.G. Hunt, J. Antonakis, K.B. Boal, with N. Lane (eds), *Being There Even When You Are Not, Leading through Strategy, Structures, and Systems: Monographs in Leadership and Management, Vol. 4.* Bingley: Emerald Publishing, pp. 105–26.

Shin, T. (2012) 'The gender gap in executive compensation: the role of female directors and chief executive officers', *The Annals of the American Academy of Political and Social Science*, 639 (1): 258–78.

Shotter, J. (1993) *Conversational Realities: Constructing Life through Language.* London: Sage.

Shotter, J. and Cunliffe, A.L. (2002) 'Managers as practical authors: everyday conversations for action', in D. Holman and R. Thorpe (eds), *Management and Language: The Manager as Practical Author.* London: Sage, pp. 15–37.

Sims, D. (2003) 'Between the millstones: a narrative account of the vulnerability of middle managers' storytelling', *Human Relations*, 56 (10): 1195–211.

Sims, D. (2008) 'Managerial identity formation in a public sector professional: an autobiographical account', *International Journal of Public Administration*, 31 (9): 988–1002.

Skivenes, M. and Trygstad, S.C. (2010) 'When whistle-blowing works: the Norwegian case', *Human Relations*, 63 (7): 1071–97.

Spivak, G.C. (1999) *A Critique of Postcolonial Reason: Toward a History of the Vanishing Present.* Cambridge, MA: Harvard University Press.

Stein, M. (2011) 'A culture of mania: a psychoanalytical view of the incubation of the 2008 credit crisis', *Organization*, 18 (2): 173–86.

Stewart, R. (1967) *Managers and Their Jobs* . Maidenhead: McGraw-Hill

Stewart, R. (1976) *Contrasts in Management.* Maidenhead: McGraw-Hill.

Stewart, R. (1982) *Choices for the Manager.* Englewood Cliffs, NJ: Prentice-Hall.

Tannen, D. (1995) *Gender and Discourse.* Oxford: Oxford University Press.

Tannen, D. (2001) *Talking from 9 to 5: Women and Men at Work.* New York: Harper Collins Paperbacks.

Taylor, C. (2004) *Modern Social Imaginaries.* Durham, NC: Duke University Press.

Taylor, F.W. (1911) *The Principles of Scientific Management*. New York: Harper.

Thadhani, R. (2005) 'Between monocles and veils: glimpses in postcolonial public administration', *International Journal of Public Administration*, 28 (11/12): 973–88.

Thomas, R. and Davis, A. (2005) 'Theorizing the micro-politics of resistance: New Public Management and managerial identities in the UK public services', *Organization Studies*, 25 (6): 683–706.

Thomas, R. and Linstead, A. (2002) 'Losing the plot? Middle managers and identity', *Organization*, 9 (1): 71–93.

Thomas, R., Sargent, L.D. and Hardy, C. (2011) 'Managing organizational change: negotiating meaning and power-resistance relations', *Organization Science*, 22 (1): 22–41.

Tracy, S.J. (2000) 'Becoming a character for commerce: emotion labor, self-subordination, and discursive construction of identity in a total institution', *Management Communication Quarterly*, 14 (1): 90–128.

Vaill, P.B. (1989) *Managing as a Performing Art: New Ideas for a World of Chaotic Change*. San Francisco: Jossey-Bass.

Verhezen, P. (2010) 'Giving voice in a culture of silence: from a culture of compliance to a culture of integrity', *Journal of Business Ethics*, 96 (2): 187–206.

Ward, J. and McMurray, R. (2011) 'The unspoken work of general practitioner receptionists: a re-examination of emotion management in primary care', *Social Science and Medicine*, 72 (10): 1583–7.

Warhurst, R. (2011) 'Managers' practice and managers' learning as identity formation: reassessing the MBA contribution', *Management Learning*, 42 (3): 261–78.

Watson, T.J. (2001) *In Search of Management: Culture, Chaos and Control in Managerial Work*. London: Routledge [first published 1994].

Watson, T.J. (2008) 'Managing identity: identity work, personal predicaments and structural circumstances', *Organization*, 15 (1): 121–43.

Watson, T.J. (2009) 'Narrative life story and the management of identity: a case study in autobiographical identity work', *Human Relations*, 62 (3): 1–28.

Watson, T.J. (2011) 'Ethnography, reality and truth: the vital need for studies of "how things work" in organisations and management', *Journal of Management Studies*, 48 (1): 202–17.

Watson, T.J. and Harris, P. (1999) *The Emergent Manager*. London: Sage.

Weber, M. (1947) *The Theory of Social and Economic Organization*, ed. A. H. Henderson and T. Parsons. Glencoe, IL: Free Press [first published 1924].

Weick, K.E. (1995) *Sensemaking in Organizations*. London: Sage.

Weick, K.E. (2001) *Making Sense of the Organization*. Oxford: Blackwell Publishers.

Weick, K.E. (2007) 'The generative properties of richness', *Academy of Management Journal*, 50 (1): 14–19.

Welsh, M.A. and Dehler, G.E. (2007) 'Whither the MBA? Or the withering of MBAs?', *Management Learning*, 38 (4): 405–23.

Whetton, D.A. and Cameron, K.S. (1983) 'Management skill training: a needed addition to the management curriculum', *Exchange: The Organizational Behavior Teaching Journal*, 8 (2): 10–15.

Whittle A. and Mueller, F. (2012) 'Bankers in the dock: moral storytelling in action', *Human Relations*, 65 (1): 111–39.

Wilensky, H.L. (1964) 'The professionalization of everyone?', *American Journal of Sociology*, 70 (2): 137–58.

Willmott, H. (1994) 'Management education, provocations to a debate', *Management Learning*, 25 (1): 105–36.

Willmott, H. (1998) 'Towards a new ethics? The contributions of post-structuralism and posthumanism', in M. Parker (ed.), *Ethics and Organizations*. London: Sage, pp. 76–121.

Winn, M.I and Pogutz, S. (2013) 'Business, ecosystems, and biodiversity: new horizons for management research', *Organization & Environment*, 26 (2): 203–29.

Zukin, S. (1996) *The Cultures of Cities*. Malden, MA: Blackwell Publishers.

# Additional Reading

Alvesson, M. (2013) *Understanding Organizational Culture* (2nd edn). London: Sage.

Alvesson, M. and Kärreman, D. (2011) 'Decolonizing discourse: critical reflections on organizational discourse analysis', *Human Relations*, 64 (9): 1121–46.

Beech, N. (2008) 'On the nature of dialogic identity work', *Organization*, 15 (1): 51–74.

Bell, E. and King, D. (2010) 'The elephant in the room: critical management studies conferences as a site of body pedagogics', *Management Learning*, 41 (4): 429–42.

Boje, D.M. (1995) 'Stories of the storytelling organization: a postmodern analysis of Disney as Tamara-land', *Academy of Management Journal*, 38 (4): 997–1035.

Brenna, N.M. and Conroy, J.P. (2013) 'Executive hubris: the case of a bank CEO', *Accounting, Auditing and Accountability Journal*, 26 (2): 172–95.

Cain, C. (2012) 'Integrating dark humor and compassion: identities and presentations of self in the front and back regions of hospice', *Journal of Contemporary Ethnography*, 41 (6): 668–94.

Clegg, S., Pitsis, T. and Kornberger, M. (2008) *Managing and Organizations: An Introduction to Theory and Practice*. London: Sage.

Clegg, S.R. and van Iterson, A. (2009) 'Dishing the dirt: gossiping in organizations', *Culture and Organization*, 15 (3–4): 275–89.

Collinson, D. (1992) *Managing the Shopfloor: Subjectivity, Masculinity and Workplace Culture*. Berlin: De Gruyter.

Collinson, D. and Hearn, M. (eds) (1997) *Men as Managers, Managers as Men: Critical Perspectives on Men, Masculinities and Management*. London: Sage.

Corlett, S. (2013) 'Participant learning in and through research as reflexive dialogue: being "struck" and the effects of recall', *Management Learning*. Epub ahead of print, 6 August 2012. DOI:10.1177/1350 507612453429

Cunliffe A.L. (2004) 'On becoming a critically reflexive practitioner', *Journal of Management Education*, 28 (4): 407–26.

Cunliffe, A.L. and Jun, J. (2005) 'The need for reflexivity in public administration', *Administration and Society*, 37 (2): 225–42.

Currie, D. and McElwee, G. (2009) '"I've got those empty diary blues": a wee case study of performance management in a Glasgow office',

*Tamara, Journal of Critical Postmodern Organization Science*, 8 (1): 59–72.

Donaldson, L. (2008) 'Ethics problems and problems with ethics: toward a pro-management theory', *Journal of Business Ethics*, 78 (3): 299–311.

Down, S. and Reveley, J. (2009) 'Between narration and interaction: situating first-line supervisor identity work', *Human Relations*, 62 (3): 379–401.

Fairhurst, G. (2007) *Discursive Leadership: In Conversation with Leadership Psychology*. Thousand Oaks, CA: Sage.

Fotaki, M. and Harding, N. (2013) 'Lacan and sexual difference in organization and management theory: towards a hysterical academy?', *Organization*, 20 (2): 153–72.

Foucault, M. (1977) *Discipline and Punish: The Birth of the Prison*. London: Penguin.

Fougère, M. and Moulettes, A. (2012) 'Disclaimers, dichotomies and disappearances in international business textbooks: a postcolonial deconstruction', *Management Learning*, 43 (1): 5–24.

Fournier, V. and Keleman, M. (2001) 'The crafting of community: recoupling discourses of management and womanhood', *Gender, Work and Organization*, 8 (3): 267–90.

Gagliardi, P. (ed.) (1990) *Symbols and Artifacts: Views of the Corporate Landscape*. Berlin and New York: de Gruyter.

Gergen, K.J. (2009) *Relational Being: Beyond Self and Community*. New York: Oxford University Press.

Grey, C. (1996) 'Towards a critique of managerialism: the contribution of Simon Weil', *Journal of Management Studies*, 33 (5): 591–611.

Harding, N. (2002) 'On the manager's body as an aesthetics of control', *Tamara, Journal of Critical Postmodern Organization Science*, 2 (1): 63–76.

Hay, A. (2013) '"I don't know what I am doing!": surfacing struggles of managerial identity work', *Management Learning*. Epub ahead of print, 13 May 2013 DOI:10.1177/1350507613483421.

Heidegger, M. (1978) *Basic Writings*, ed. D.F. Krell. London: Routledge.

Holt, R. (2006) 'Principles and practice: rhetoric and the moral character of managers', *Human Relations*, 59 (12): 1659–80.

Imas J.M. and Weston, A. (2012) 'From Harare to Rio de Janeiro: Kukiya-Favela organization of the excluded', *Organization*, 19 (2): 205–27.

Johansson, U. and Woodilla, J. (2005) *Irony and Organizations: Epistemological Claims and Supporting Field Stories*. Malmö, Sweden: Liber.

Kanter, R.M. (1977) *Men and Women of the Corporation*. New York: Basic Books.

Kärreman, D. (2001) 'The scripted organization: dramaturgy from Burke to Baudrillard', in R. Westwood and S. Linstead (eds), *The Language of Organization*. London: Sage, pp. 89–111.

Kociatkiewicz, J. and Kostera, M. (2012) 'The good manager: an archetypical quest for morally sustainable leadership', *Organization Studies*, 33 (7): 861–78.

Lutgen-Sandvik, P. (2008) 'Intensive remedial identity work: responses to workplace bullying trauma and stigmatization', *Organization*, 15 (1): 97–119.

Manning, P.K. (2008) 'Goffman on organizations', *Organization Studies*, 29 (5): 677–99.

Martin, D.M. (2004) 'Humor in middle management: women negotiating the paradoxes of organizational life', *Journal of Applied Communication Research*, 32 (2): 147–70.

Mirchandani, K. (2003) 'Challenging racial silences in studies of emotion work: contributions from anti-racist feminist theory', *Organization Studies*, 24 (5): 721–42.

Mumby, D. (1998) 'Organizing men: power, discourse and the social construction of masculinity(s) in the workplace', *Communication Theory*, 8 (2): 164–83.

Prasad, A. (ed.) (2003) *Postcolonial Theory and Organization Analysis: A Critical Engagement*. New York: Palgrave Macmillan.

Rowland, W. (2009) 'Reflections on metaphor and identity in the cybercorporation', *Journal of Business Ethics*, 94 (3): 15–12.

Rowlinson, M., Toms, S. and Wilson, J.F. (2007) 'Competing perspectives on the "managerial revolution": from "managerialist" to "antimanagerialist"', *Business History*, 49 (4): 464–82.

Sartre, J.-P. (1965) *Essays in Existentialism*. New York: Citadel Press, Kensington Publishing [reprinted 1993].

Simon, H. (1955) 'A behavioral model of rational choice', *Quarterly Journal of Economics*, 69 (1): 99–118.

Sveningsson, S. and Alvesson, M. (2003) 'Managing managerial identities: organizational fragmentation, discourse and identity struggle', *Human Relations*, 56 (10): 1163–93.

Van Iterson, A., Waddington, K. and Michelson, G. (2011) 'Breaking the silence: the role of gossip in organizational culture', in N.M. Ashkanasy, C.P.M. Wilderom and M.F. Peterson (eds), *The Handbook of Organizational Culture and Climate*. Thousand Oaks, CA: Sage, pp. 375–92.

Westwood, R. and Johnston, A. (2012) 'Reclaiming authentic selves: control, resistive humour and identity work in the office', *Organization*, 19 (6): 787–808.

Whittington, R. (2006) 'Completing the practice turn in strategy research', *Organization Studies*, 27 (5): 613–34.

Zanoni, P. and Janssens, M. (2004) 'Deconstructing difference: the rhetorics of HR managers' diversity discourses', *Organization Studies*, 25 (1): 55–74.

# Index